TRAVEL AGENCY:

A How-to-Do-It Manual for Starting One of Your Own

TRAVEL AGENCY:

A How-to-Do-It Manual for Starting One of Your Own

by Anne Stenholm

Published by Freelance Publications, Bayport, NY

Copyright 1979 by Anne Stenholm

All rights reserved including the right of reproduction in whole or in part in any form

Library of Congress Catalog Card Number: 78-67643
ISBN: 0-9602050-0-4

Typeset by Anne Stenholm

Printed by Wampeter Press

Published by Freelance Publications
P.O. Box 8, Bayport, NY, 11705

Manufactured in U.S.A.

*This book is dedicated to
my mother—the original Anne Stenholm*

TABLE OF CONTENTS

About This Book..................................*11*

INTRODUCTION........................ *13—22*
    The Appeal of the Travel Business, 13
    What a Travel Agency Is and Does, 14
    Definitions and Abbreviations, 14
    Pros and Cons of Owning a Travel Agency, 14
    The Airline Conferences, 15
    Conference Requirements, 16
    Aims and Intent of This Manual, 16

PHASE ONE—*The All-Important Preliminaries*......... *23—36*
    Read for an Overview, 23
    Get Started, 24
    A Personal Reading List, 24
    Take Notes as you Read, 25
    Organize the Information, 25
    Read the Trade Press, 26
    Financial and Legal Advice, 26
    Estimate Capital Requirements, 27
    Hire a Consultant?, 27
    The SBA, 28
    Some Skills You'll Need, 28
    Information Sources and Resources, 29
    Working Techniques, 29
    Goals for Phase One, 29

PHASE TWO—Legal/Financial Matters .... 37—48
    Conference Application Kits, 37
    Understand their Contents, 38
    Interpreting Conference Requirements, 38
    Hire Your Lawyer and Accountant, 39
    Working With Experts, 40
    Choosing a Legal Structure for the Agency, 40
    Partners and Partnerships, 41
    A Partner as the ERP, 42
    The Parnership Agreement, 42
    A Name and a Logo, 43
    Financial Commitments and a Working Budget, 43
    Winding Up Phase Two, 44
    Start a Draft of the Applications, 44

PHASE THREE—Premises and Personnel .... 49—60
    Specifications for Premises and Personnel, 49
    Techniques for Finding Them, 50
    Deciding on a Location, 51
    Minimum Staffing Requirements, 51
    Importance of the ERP You Choose, 52
    The Lease and Employee Contracts, 53
    A Things-To-Do List, 53
    Select Your Bank, 54
    Designing and Decorating the Office, 55

PHASE FOUR—Sales: Set-up and Promotion .... 61—70
    Get Ready for Travel Sales, 61
    Plan a Sales Promotion Campaign, 62
    IATA Guidelines for Sales Promotion, 63
    Coordination and Deadlines, 64
    Agency Policies and Procedures, 65
    Air Travel Sales, 65
    Set Up a Filing System, 66
    Start a Bookkeeping System, 66
    Compile a Mailing List, 66
    An Open House Party, 67

PHASE FIVE—Application for Appointment .... 71—79
    The ATC Application, 72
    The IATA Application, 73
    What Happens Now?, 75
    Sales Productivity, 75
    Living in Limbo, 76
    A Few Last Details, 78
    Final Note, 78

EXHIBITS

1—Definitions and Abbreviations	*19-22*
2—ATC Letter of Instructions	*30-34*
3—Suggestions for Using the Library System and Recording Notes and Information	*35, 36*
4—Checklist for Estimating Capital Requirements	*45*
5—What is a Travel Agency Worth?	*46, 47*
6—Checklist for Planning a Working Budget	*48*
7—Checklist for Setting Standards and Evaluating Agency Premises and Location	*56, 57*
8—Checklist for Setting Standards, Interviewing, Hiring of Staff and for Devising an Application Form	*58, 59*
9—Checklist for Remodeling and/or Redecorating Office Space	*60*
10—Checklist for Setting Up for Office Operations and Travel Sales	*69, 70*
11—Checklist for Assembling Applications for Appointment	*79*

APPENDICES

A—Suggestions for Further Reading and Study	*81-86*
B—Information Sources and Resources	*87-90*
C—Airline Conference Application Information	*91-119*

About this book—

This is a practical Manual and workbook which organizes the process of starting a new travel agency into a series of phases and steps. It is intended for the complete novice, as well as for working travel agents who dream of some day starting travel agencies of their own. And it's the book I wish had been available to me a couple of years ago when I first became involved in starting a new agency.

The Manual is based on my own experience in that venture, but has its roots in a college paper I researched at a time when the idea of starting a travel agency was only in terms of a possible new career for retirement years.

I had enrolled in one of the non-traditional colleges especially hospitable to older women like me. As a new student I had to research and write a paper on career goals and the kind of degree program I would want to help fulfill those goals. In exploring the various fields that appealed to me, I was struck by the skimpy number of books available on starting and operating a travel agency. It seemed to me then— and does now—that there ought to be more material available, especially from the viewpoint of the small agency operator. And why weren't there more such books?

Anyway, I did manage to finish the research paper and began a series of independent studies in travel agency management, along with the usual liberal arts courses.

Less than a year later, what had been a long-range retirement plan suddenly was an immediate activity when a travel agent friend asked if I'd like to join her and start a new agency now, rather than in the vague future.

Even though this meant a total shift in plans, and was premature in terms of my studies, I decided to go ahead.

In the back of my head, however, from the very beginning, I had in mind that the venture might also provide the subject for the kind of how-to-do-it book I'd not been able to find. Therefore, I took notes as I went along—both factual and subjective—resurrected the file on that college paper I had written, expanded and updated the research notes, and put together this Manual.

Its intent is to provide an introductory book and working manual for readers who are totally new to the industry, as well as for travel industry employees who may be considering moving upward into travel agency ownership.

It is written from the viewpoint of one who, as a novice, has recently been through the process of starting a new agency. If, at times, the tone seems overly cautionary that is the result of missteps I feel I made, which having been forewarned, you may be able to avoid.

—Anne Stenholm

Introduction

If you're reading this book, chances are—

- you're a travel agent (or an outside sales rep) with a longing to some day have a travel agency of your own, or
- you're an ardent traveler, with the financial wherewithall and a yen to use all your travel experience in a new career, or
- you perhaps now own some kind of small business such as a beauty shop or real estate agency, and want to take a flier into something new and something that seems far more exciting than what you're doing now

The Appeal of the Travel Business

There's no doubt that owning a travel agency has a glamor image these days. It sounds like great fun to deal in such a happy commodity as travel and to have all those free travel benefits that come with owning an agency.

Like most popular images, however, the truth includes some less glamorous factors. Owning a travel agency involves all the problems and frustrations of owning any small business. And there are a few special problems and frustrations peculiar only to the travel business.

Still, for those bitten by the bug, any disadvantages seem to be offset by the persistent ambition to open another brand new travel agency. The phenomenal growth in the number of new agencies is evidence of this and the trend does not appear to be diminishing.

What a Travel Agency Is and Does

A travel agency sells travel services to its clientele. It represents virtually all travel suppliers (or principals as they are sometimes called) and acts as a middleman between the supplier and the individual who needs or wants to travel. The supplier expects and hopes the travel agency will promote and sell its product, yet the customer expects unbiased advice in choosing which travel product to buy. A conflicting role? To a degree it is—much like the role of a stockbroker who can sell many stocks, but tries to choose those which best serve his client's needs.

So while the travel agency represents the various suppliers, it must do so in a way that will result in satisfied customers who return to that travel agency again and again.

A travel agency's services are free for the most part. It is the suppliers and principals who provide the agency's income by paying varying rates of commission for travel sales made through that agency.

Definitions and Abbreviations

Exhibit 1, at the end of this Introduction, defines some of the terms and abbreviations used in the travel industry. If you are new to the field, put a marker at this page until the definitions are familiar to you.

Pros and Cons of Owning a Travel Agency

The reading you'll do, as part of this Manual's approach to starting a travel agency, should help decide whether or not this is the business for you. Here's just a brief list of the most obvious pros and cons.

The pros—
- Less capital required than for many small businesses because there's no inventory to carry
- Rewarding work with new things to learn and new places to visit a constant factor
- Many opportunities for reduced price travel
- A happy business—people want to travel and need your services
- A growing business with tremendous future growth potential—people having more leisure and more disposable income

The cons—
- Relative ease of entry into the business makes for an intensely competitive situation; many areas are saturated with agencies
- Much tedious clerical work; exacting work and endless details
- Profit margin is low compared to most businesses
- The travel "freebees" are not nearly as liberal as the public believes
- Travel sales are greatly affected by conditions beyond the control of the agency owner—political upheavals in any part of the world, Federal regulations, etc.
- Travel agencies are legally vulnerable, in many cases for failures in delivery of travel services that are not their fault at all

The Airline Conferences

Earning the right to operate a travel agency basically means satisfying ATC and IATA, the two conferences to which most domestic and international airlines belong. You cannot stock and write airline tickets until they appoint you to the Agency List, and you cannot really operate a travel agency unless you can sell air travel.

True, there are retail travel agencies that deal only in packaged tours, or operate a specialized agency that doesn't require airline ticket sales. These are the exception, however, and are not the kind of full-service, department store of travel, we usually think of when we use the term travel agency.

You must be open for business, fully staffed and equipped, BEFORE you even file for your appointment to the Agency List. In other words, you must be prepared to invest a great deal of time, money and effort, without any guarantee that your agency will ultimately qualify for addition to the List.

After filing your applications, there is a period of six weeks to three months during which you will be inspected, your references and financial status checked, and your staff investigated. This can be an anxious time. No matter how meticulously you've handled the details of filing your applications and fulfilling requirements, there is still a nagging worry until those appointments come through.

On the bright side, the ATC and IATA requirements are quite specifically stated for the most part. They are not at all unreasonable in my opinion, and you cannot be turned down by ATC capriciously. There is an appeals process to insure you will be equitably evaluated. Usually IATA will concur in approving your application once ATC has done so.

During this interim period you can sell and promote travel and earn commissions. Air sales commissions, however, must be collected retroactively upon your appointment and you will be inconvenienced by not being able to actually stock airline tickets in your office until you've been appointed.

Conference Requirements

The application forms used by ATC and IATA are quite different, and their requirements for appointment vary in detail. They can be summed up, however, as follows:
- A suitable location (or premises as IATA terms it), devoted to the sale of travel and identified as such
  Owner(s) who are bondable and bonded for a minimum of $10,000
- Provide a net worth of $20,000 of which $15,000 must be maintained as working capital
- A full-time staff that meets experience requirements of 1 year in airline ticketing and 2 years in selling and promoting travel—experience requirements may be met by one or more persons who may be owners or employees
- Applicant must demonstrate the "ability and willingness to promote and advertise" travel and provide samples of ads, direct mail pieces, promotion, etc.

There are other details regarding security, photographs of the premises, reference letters, and so on, but the above list covers the major requirements.

Aims and Intent of this Manual

In my preface to this book, I mentioned that I had found an odd scarcity of material on travel agency ownership when I had researched for such material a few years ago. At least it seemed odd to a library buff like me when I considered the flood of how-to-do-its published every year, on every imaginable subject. And travel,as well as travel agencies are, in my view a "trendy" subject, about which one would logically expect a steady flow of new books.

Once you are part of the industry, as an employee or as an owner, there is a wealth of material available. But for the newcomer, on the outside, you'll find little at your local library.

I think I know the reason for it, and it is a simple one. Travel agency owners, once in business themselves, don't want to give anyone else the idea, or the encouragement, to start yet another new travel agency. No more complicated than that.

While this attitude is perfectly understandable in view of the highly competitive nature of the business, I don't think this "if we don't tell 'em they won't try it" approach has had any effect at all. In fact it may contribute to the ever-growing number of new agencies. There's something about those gorgeous brochures and upbeat atmosphere that makes running a travel agency look like a fun thing to do. And the absence of an easily available, wide range of literature on the subject, makes it difficult for the potential newcomer to explore the field adequately before taking the plunge.

Of course you readers who are now travel agents, or outside sales reps, do have a far more down-to-earth view of the business than those of you whose only travel industry exposure has been that of the enthusiastic amateur traveler.

However, your general business knowledge and awareness of small business problems could be as deficient as that of the total newcomer. A story I heard at a ticketing seminar illustrates the point exactly.

The owner of a prosperous suburban travel agency decided to retire. Before putting the agency up for sale, she decided to give her long-time agency manager the first opportunity to buy it. The manager bought the agency to the delight of all including the employees who could now stay on as before.

The manager had run the agency for years and you would think this an ideal transition. But not so. The investment of his life's savings plus debts incurred in taking over the agency, plus the absence of the good judgment of the departed owner, turned an excellent employee-manager into a carping, hypercritical boss who resented every paper clip used and questioned every move his staff made in handling travel sales.

Eventually, he drove almost his entire staff into the arms of nearby competitors.

Now why this unexpected result? To me it simply points up the difference between being an employee (no matter how experienced) and an employer and business owner. Therefore, the travel agent, or outside sales rep, needs to explore the realities of actually owning a travel agency just as much as does the total newcomer to the travel industry.

The intent of this Manual, then, is to provide its readers with a step-by-step guide, and a source of further reading and exploration. Its aim is also to convince you to approach the idea of starting a travel agency with much respect and to allow sufficient time for the self-assessment, self-education, and inquiries dealt with in Phase One.

Did we follow all the steps I list, do all the reading I recommend, take all the precautions suggested? No we did not—but we should have!

A final note before starting Phase One. If you live in a state which already has laws on the books governing the establishment of travel agencies, those specific procedures must be followed IN ADDITION TO the steps included in this Manual.

EXHIBIT 1

DEFINITIONS AND ABBREVIATIONS

This is a brief list of the most common definitions and abbreviations used in the travel industry and incorporated in this Manual. For a more complete listing, obtain a copy of The ABCs of Travel (see Appendix B, under Reference Books and Subscriptions).

agency list—Promulgated by the two air traffic conferences. Acceptance on the list means that you have been approved and appointed by these two conferences to act as their agent and to maintain airline ticket stock in your agency office.

airline rep—The sales representative for an airline. The travel agency's personal contact with the airline to help with problems, promotional materials, general sales assistance.

AMTRAK—The organization which operates most railroads in the U.S. other than commuter lines, with the official name of the National Railroad Passenger Corporation. As a travel agency you may decide to seek "appointment" as an agent of AMTRAK and to carry their ticket stock.

appointment(s)—Status conferred on a travel agency by the airlines, but which may also include IPSA, TPPC and AMTRAK. To speak of a "fully appointed agency" means an agency that has these appointments and can operate as a full service travel agency. For the purpose of this book, however, when I refer to "appointments" I mean ATC and IATA appointments.

Area Bank—The airline conference clearing house through which airline ticket sales are funneled, and individual airlines reimbursed.

ARTA—Association of Retail Travel Agents, a trade association of retail travel agency owners and employees of retail travel agencies.

ASTA—The American Society of Travel Agents, the largest and most influential trade association, includes retail and wholesale owners, as well as representatives of various principals. Not open to employees of retail travel agencies.

ATC—Air Traffic Conference, the unit of the air transportation hierarchy most directly in control of travel agencies and agents, their establishment and their dealings with the industry and traveling public. ATC is composed of domestic air carriers and, with the Federal regulatory agencies, provides a unified system of air travel within the U.S.

bond, bonding—A minimum bond of $10,000 is required by ATC as an indication of financial integrity before a travel agency can be appointed as an agent for domestic airline travel sales. Maintenance of the bond is a continuing requirement and the bond must increase in proportion to the agency's annual air travel sales.

CAB—ATC's superior in the air travel hierarchy. This is a Federal regulatory agency which licenses airlines as carriers, approves schedules, rates, etc. and to which ATC must apply for changes in regulations dealing with retail travel agencies.

EXHIBIT 1, continued

conferences—These are organizations which represent a group of principals or companies who provide various travel products. The ATC represents domestic airlines; IATA represents international airlines; IPSA represents cruise lines and ships operating from eastern ports; TPPC represents western port companies. Not every principal or company in an industry necessarily belongs to a conference, however. For instance, at this writing Pan Am had withdrawn from IATA. This fact means little to the retail travel agency; you are basically beholden to conference rules and regulations and must apply to the conference for appointment. Individual members of each conference do not have to recognize you as their individual agent, but ordinarily they will accept any travel agency which has been approved by the conference.

errors and omissions insurance—travel industry insurance which, as its name indicates, offers protection to a travel agency from liability, or limits liability, for certain errors and omissions in dealing with its clientele. Whether your agency can purchase such insurance is something which must be individually checked.

ERP—Simply an acronym I made up for this Manual, for brevity's sake, to designate the person, or persons, in an agency meeting airline conference requirements for appointment. It means the "experience requirement person" or persons you list in the ATC application.

exchange order—A form used to request issuance of an airline ticket (or other travel service). During the period between filing the applications for appointment by the airline conferences, and the date of appointment, you may be required to use this form in dealing with individual airlines and handling airline ticket sales.

fam trip—Industry abbreviation for "familiarization trip" which is an educational and/or promotional trip, organized by principals, and offered to travel agency personnel on a reduced rate, or free, basis.

IATA—International Air Transport Association. With ATC, this is the second key organization involved in the appointment of a travel agency. It does for international airlines what the ATC does for domestic lines, in order to provide a unified system of air transport services to the traveling public. It is a supra-national organization.

ICTA—Institute of Certified Travel Agents. A travel industry educational organization that is endeavoring to professionalize and upgrade the educational level of travel agents and agencies. ICTA devises, coordinates, and administers an education and testing program geared particularly to the travel agency owner-manager, and leading to the designation of "Certified Travel Counselor" (CTC).

IPSA—International Passenger Ship Association. The conference of ships and cruise lines generally operating from eastern ports and on the Atlantic Ocean. This Manual is primarily concerned with appointment by the airline conferences; application should also be submitted to IPSA, however.

EXHIBIT 1, continued

mechanized reporting system—Part of the system for transmitting payment for airline travel sales. You are required to submit weekly airline ticket sales reports; the area bank then is authorized to draw against your bank for payment of reported sales which monies are then transmitted to the airlines. Most agencies set up a special ATC checking account to handle their air travel ticket sales.

media—Any means of communication through which you advertise, publicize, or promote your agency or what it sells. It could be local newspapers, radio, direct mail promotion, brochures, TV, a newsletter—whatever.

premises—IATA's term for your place of business as a travel agency. In this Manual used interchangeably at times with "location" or "agency location."

principals—Indicates the wholesalers, suppliers, tour operators, etc. who provide the travel services you sell as a retail agency.

references—The body of knowledge available to travel agencies for counseling and serving their clientele. Includes tariffs, manuals, reference guides, subscription services, guidebooks, brochures, etc.

retail travel agency—The type of agency for which this Manual is intended which, for the most part, sells the products of wholesalers and other travel industry principals.

RRT—Means "reduced rate transportation" and refers to the special rate air travel granted by ATC and IATA to appointed travel agencies after a waiting period of one year. Rules and procedures for taking advantage of this travel are rigid and somewhat complicated. At this writing, there is a movement on the part of agencies to give up the privilege in exchange for a higher commission rate on air ticket sales.

tariff—Fares, or rates, or any publication listing fares and rates.

tour operator—The travel industry principal which plans, finances and contracts for the myriad services involved in a tour package. Tour operators are usually wholesalers, but sometimes do sell their product directly to travelers as well as through retail travel agencies. A retail agency stocks brochures and sells the products of a wide variety of tour operators. A key factor in operating an agency is having a staff that knows which tour operators are responsible and ethical and can be relied upon to deliver the package promised in the brochures.

TPPC—Transpacific Passenger Conference, the Pacific Ocean and western port counterpart of IPSA. Once a travel agency has been appointed by the airlines, it should also apply to TPPC for appointment.

USTOA—United States Tour Operators Association. USTOA has strict requirements for membership as to financial stability, reputation, expertise, etc. in organizing and advertising tours. Thus, dealing with a tour operator who is also a USTOA member does offer some security for the retail travel agency. However many leading, established, tour operators, with impeccable reputations, do not belong to USTOA.

EXHIBIT 1, continued

validator—The mechanical device used to validate airline tickets (similar to the validation the sales girl does when you use your charge plate at a department store). Upon appointment you will receive your agency plate, and then each airline will provide individual plates, to use in the validator.

wholesaler—A company that develops a travel product which is then sold through retail travel agencies. Wholesalers operate under many rules and regulations that do not apply to retailers, and this type of operation is not the concern of this Manual.

Phase One

The All-Important Preliminaries

I've tried to organize this Manual sequentially. That is, I've tried to put one step or process after the next in logical, and chronological, fashion. This is the way it all ought to happen. In actual practice, however, you'll probably find yourself zig-zagging at times, coming to a dead stop now and then due to unforseen circumstances, and working on particular items out of the numbered order given here.

The best approach, then, is to use this Manual to keep from making gross mistakes in timing. Be flexible enough, however, to jump ahead when circumstances make it practical to do so, going back later to handle any skipped items.

Read for an Overview

Begin by reading through the Manual quickly to familiarize yourself with its general contents and to get an overview of what is involved. Don't stop at this point to do any of the supplementary reading and investigation.

Phase One is an information gathering and learning phase—those all-important preliminaries.

Phase Two deals with financial/legal matters and ends when you've established your forthcoming travel agency as a legal entity.

Three and Four are concerned with meeting Conference requirements as to location, staff, sales operations and promotion.

Phase Five begins when you're ready to open your doors for business and file the applications for appointment with ATC and IATA.

The Exhibits at the close of each section, and the Appendices at the back of the Manual, are an essential part of this book, and as important as the main text. They contain the checklists, resource information, addresses, etc., I felt were necessary if the Manual is to serve as a practical workbook.

Get Started

Getting started involves writing a few letters and finding out what your library has to offer in the way of free information:

1) Send to IATA and ATC for current information on appointing a new travel agency. You'll receive information and applications from IATA, but only a letter from ATC. You must include a $10 check if you want the ATC application kit. Appendix C has excerpts of the kit to use for the time being until you decide you are definitely going to open an agency. At that point you would have to request the $10 kit.

2) Send to each of the bonding companies listed in Appendix B and any others you may want to contact, for their application for a bond. Explain that it will be to satisfy ATC's requirement for a travel agency.

3) Look up every book listed in Appendix A in the card catalog of your local library, or any other nearby libraries you may have access to. Note the card catalog number and where it is shelved. For those books not available locally, find out from the librarian the procedure for obtaining them through the inter-library loan system. You can also stop by the library of nearby colleges. They may permit use of their facilities if you ask, or they may at least let you examine and read books there.

A Personal Reading List

How much supplementary reading and study you do as part of Phase One depends on your general business experience, travel industry experience, and how important you think such pre-study is. As the very minimum, I would read (and re-read) the following, whether your library has them or not. The investment involved is really very little if you are serious about starting a travel agency:

Guide to Buying, Selling and Starting a Travel Agency by Laurence Stevens
Travel Agency Management by Brownell
Exhibit 2, herein
The SBA publication on starting a small business, plus one or two others on the subject

Once you've made a firm decision to go ahead, then a thorough reading and understanding of both the ATC and IATA applications and enclosures is essential.

Appendix A has additional notes on sources of general and special information you may wish to add to your personal reading and study plan.

Take Notes as you Read

It may seem like a lot of work to take notes as you read, especially if you've never had occasion to do it before. But in my opinion, for this sort of a research and study project, it is a waste of time to read without taking notes. In the long run you will spend far more time later on trying to recall where you saw that bit of information you now need, than if you noted it down in the first place.

Because I think it is important, I've included an outline of the notetaking system I use, as Exhibit 3. If you have a better one of your own, by all means use it.

Organize the Information

Next you need to acquire a file cabinet, or at least an oversized file box, and set up a system for storing the applications and other information you will gradually acquire. The following headings are suggested for a start—later you can add as many sub-heads as necessary.

    Financial/Legal
    Location/Premises
    Staffing/Personnel
    Office Operations
    Promotion/Advertising

Read the Trade Press

If you are already working in the industry, start reading any items you see regarding appointments and possible changes in requirements for new agencies. Appendix C reflects application procedures as of January 1979, but changes are made from time to time and you should try to be aware of them, and any being considered.

If you are a newcomer to the field, you may find it difficult or impossible to obtain a subscription to any of the trade magazines until you have a registered name and address.

Financial and Legal Advice

Start thinking about who you will use for your lawyer and accountant in setting up your agency. Finding a lawyer and an accountant you can trust and afford and like is one of the major preliminary decisions you have to make.

You need the lawyer throughout opening-up procedures and afterwards, to—
- Set up the legal structure for your business (sole proprietorship, partnership, corporation)
- Advise on local licensing, zoning and registration laws for businesses in your area
- Interpret any parts of the agency sales agreements you must execute for the Conferences that are not clear
- Negotiate a lease, or sales contract, for your premises
- Give general legal advice on everying from insurance and taxes to employer/employee questions

As to an accountant—I suppose it would be technically possible to do without one, but I can't imagine doing so in these days of complicated tax laws. The accountant will advise on and handle paperwork for—
- Tax ramifications of choosing the right legal form for your business
- Capital requirements; loans, credit if needed
- Federal employment number and employee taxes
- Preparing the financial statements needed for bonding and for your Conference applications
- The bond application
- Setting up a bookkeeping system
- Income Tax Returns
- Auditing when necessary

Estimate Capital Requirements

Begin the long process of finding out what things cost so that you can make an intelligent estimate of your capital requirements. There is no book, or single information source, that can do this for you. It depends on local conditions plus the type of operation you have in mind. You will simply have to make inquiries and phone calls, check ads and catalogs, shop around, until you can arrive at a ballpark figure of what you can expect to pay for—

    Start-up Expenses
    Monthly and Annual Operational Costs

Use the lists given in Exhibit 4 as a starting point and add any other items you can think of that are unique to your area or plans.

Hire a Consultant?

I have absolutely no statistics to prove it, but I have the impression the typical, small, new travel agency owner does not seek out an industry consultant for advice. It seems to be the larger, well-established agencies which, periodically, feel the need to hire this kind of expertise. One would think the reverse would be true.

Before you reject the idea altogether, at least send away to those listed in Appendix B and find out what they would charge for the services you might want to use. In comparison to your total capital investment it may be less than you think to have the security of knowing you can call on an industry expert when there are hard decisions to be made.

One of the Small Business Administration publications I read mentioned that the unwillingness of the typical, small, entrepreneur to seek or pay for outside advice is a prime reason for the high rate of small business failures. Evidently it is part of the entrepreneural personality to want to go it alone. But if big business finds it worthwhile to hire consultants from time to time, shouldn't you at least consider the idea?

You can usually arrange to have a consultant help you with some part of the operation or act as a guide throughout the entire process. Naturally, on site advice will cost more than guidance given by letter or telephone.

The SBA

Find out where the local Small Business Administration office is in your area, and if they have a SCORE group connected with the office. The advice and information you can get is free.

SCORE is composed of volunteers who are retired business executives willing to give you the benefit of their experience. You may not be lucky enough to find a retired travel agency owner, but most of the decisions you have to make are common to all small businesses.

If your library does not stock SBA publications, you can send to the Superintendent of documents (see Appendix B) for a list of publications useful for the small business owner.

At times the SBA runs day-long seminars on small business ownership. Arrange to be notified of any such forthcoming meetings.

Some Skills You'll Need

Starting a new travel agency involves a variety of skills, other than purely travel industry knowledge, you need to have or to hire. Start considering whether you can handle them yourself, or if you have a talented relative or friend who can help you out. If you plan to use hired pros, start investigating where to locate them and what the going rate is for their services.

Here's a list of some major jobs involved in starting an agency from scratch:
- Planning an office layout and an interior design
- Choosing furnishings, a color scheme, wall and floor treatments, accessories, and so on
- Hiring and coordinating contractors, should your choice of a location require major reconstruction and/or redecorating
- Design a logo that reflects the image you want to project and possibly uses your agency name as part of the design; you'll use this logo design on stationery, cards, ads, so it is important to come up with a good one
- Planning and executing the promotion and advertising campaign that is one of IATA's requirements
  Maintaining an attractive window display area
- Typing, typing, typing—correspondence, press releases, the lengthy application forms, etc.

Information Sources and Resources

Appendix B contains lists of information and resources you will use as you work through the process of starting an agency.

Look through it from time to time and try to anticipate when various items should be sent for.

Catalogs, the Travel Industry Personnel Directory, ordering information for travel references and subscriptions, should really be on hand well before you actually use them, or you may find later you are unnecessarily inconvenienced by their absence.

Working Techniques

If you have a partner, or family and friends willing to help, avoid duplication of effort by parceling out preliminary work as much as possible. Checking out a possible office space for the first time, getting prices, screening candidates, can be one person tasks. Obviously, everyone having a financial interest in the agency will want to be part of final decisions, but the initial work can be divided up.

A combination of individual efforts, plus weekly, or twice-weekly meetings of all involved is a good way to move the whole project forward as expeditiously as possible.

Periodically, read ahead in the Manual. There may be some items on which you could be doing advance work, and you'll be that much ahead when you arrive at that Phase.

At your weekly meetings, make it a practice to keep some kind of notes on decisions made. It may seem like unnecessary work, but written notes (even if only a line in your looseleaf notebook) can avoid situations where those involved remember the discussion differently.

Goals for Phase One

Your goal, before leaving Phase One, should be to have a specific and realistic knowledge of what it takes to start and run a travel agency in terms of talents, general business acumen, travel industry knowledge, financial resources and personal qualities. You can hire people to fill any gaps, if you can afford it, but a planned "continuing education" program for yourself, is an even better idea.

EXHIBIT 2

Air Traffic Conference of America
A Division of Air Transport Association of America

1709 NEW YORK AVENUE, N. W.
WASHINGTON, D. C. 20006

This is with reference to your recent communication in which you requested information on becoming an approved travel agent for the member airlines of the Air Traffic Conference of America (ATC). 1/ If you are planning to purchase an existing agency you should keep in mind that the agency's ATC approval is not automatically transferred to the new owner and the prospective owner must meet the same requirements as any new applicant. Approval by the Air Traffic Conference is formal and represents a binding contract between the Agent and the member airlines of the Conference. Without such approval, an agent cannot receive commissions from the member airlines.

As you are undoubtedly aware, the travel industry, and particularly air passenger transportation, has entered into a new era within recent years. Since the advent of the commercial jet age air passenger transportation sales have quadrupled. By the same token, the number of ATC approved travel outlets has experienced an exceptional rate of growth. As of July 1, 1978, there were over 14,000 ATC approved travel agency locations in the United States serving over 7,200 communities. The number of locations increases 12% or more each year. With this extraordinary rate of growth has come a corresponding growth in the complexity of doing business in the travel industry for airlines and travel agents alike. New schedules, a multitude of fares, new tour offerings and other specialized travel innovations with their accompanying new procedures requires that the travel agent acquire a greater variety of knowledge and skills than ever before. Nothing evokes a client's enthusiasm like a well-planned and executed trip, nor, conversely, more wrath than the trip which did not turn out as purported by the agent.

EXHIBIT 2 (Page 2)

In this age of consumerism, law suits have become rather commonplace if tour elements are not as depicted. Accordingly, travel knowledge and travel experience are the stock in trade of the professional travel agent.

The travel agency industry is a highly specialized, intricate and unique business. If you intend to enter the travel agency field, it is important to realize that it is an exacting profession requiring specialized knowledge and skills, adequate financing, and devotion and willingness to serve the public in the best traditions of business and ethical conduct.

Before any formal action can be taken, you must submit an application in the standard format. A period of ninety (90) days should be allowed for the necessary administrative processing of a completed application. The agency location must be staffed and open for business at the time the application is submitted. During the pendency of the application, you may serve your clients by purchasing tickets directly from the airlines. Such sales will be commissionable after the final disposition of your application, and will be retro-active to the date of receipt of the complete application. In order to assist you in deciding whether you wish to submit an application to become an ATC-approved travel agent, we should like to highlight very briefly some of the requirements.

PERSONNEL QUALIFICATIONS

The principal-agent relationship was established many years ago on the airlines' belief that travel agents, through creative selling and promotional efforts, could develop a significant increment of traffic that might not otherwise travel by air. Since that time, of course, flying has become a popular and accepted way of traveling, and the travel agent has been accepted and recognized as an important part thereof. The efforts of travel agents to promote and sell, whether to new or established markets, is of equal importance today. This, obviously, is true as a business matter for the agent; but it is also an important factor in the principal's interest in continuing a strong and healthy air transport system, conveniently available to the traveling public at the lowest possible fares. These considerations point to the importance placed by the airlines on the matter of personnel who will operate and manage the agency. The requisite experience required of personnel at the outset and on a continuing basis is described in two separate and distinct categories:

    1. It is required that an owner, officer, or manager with bona fide managerial responsibility must have had at least two years of full-time experience in creating, generating and promoting passenger transportation sales and services related thereto. This type of sales experience is not to be

31

EXHIBIT 2 (Page 3)

confused with the technical experience, as set forth in #2 below, or experience servicing an already established account. The promotional sales experience referred to here means full-time experience in developing new markets, and includes such facets as advertising (media, direct mail, newspapers, etc.), conducting sales seminars, luncheon, club, church or business appearances, direct customer solicitations, and other related activities. This person must be employed on a full-time basis, and devote all of his or her time to the management and administration of the agency and to the promotion and sale of passenger transportation. Some fiscal responsibility should, of course, be included, and the agency without the availability of accounting expertise is heading for quick trouble.

2. Quite apart from the above requirement, the agency must also have an employee who has had one year's experience in airline ticketing within the past three years, with either an ATC or IATA member airline or its accredited travel agency. This requirement is directed at one's ability to compute fares, conclude all necessary reservation details in proper sequence, complete the proper ticketing forms correctly, and collect the proper amount due whether in cash, on an authorized credit plan, or a combination of both.

One person may meet both of the above requirements. In any event, appropriate evidence and resumes (including letters of reference) must be submitted with the application to demonstrate clearly that this person(s) meets the necessary standards. The air carriers place particular emphasis on the proven expertise of agency personnel and this matter demands careful consideration by anyone contemplating travel as a business. In this regard, we strongly emphasize that you contact former employers in order to ensure that your proposed "qualifier" has had the requisite experience as outlined above before you make application with ATC.

LOCATION

An applicant must have an acceptable location and be open for business at the time the application is made. The prospective agent has a responsibility to provide a convenient and attractive office to receive potential customers and to make the location of his place of business well-known in the community. Of course, the people selected to work in the office, too, should be well-known, active and responsible in the community. The agency location must be open and easily accessible to the general public during normal business hours. It must be adequately identified as a travel agency and sufficiently separated from other businesses that may be operated at the same location. An application will not be approved if

EXHIBIT 2 (Page 4)

the agent is located on airport property, nor will a location be approved if it is in a hotel, unless the agency has a street-front location with access from the street by means of a door opening directly from the street and not requiring passage through any portion of the hotel. There are also restrictions and prohibitions concerning locations in private clubs, private residences, etc.

BUSINESS WITH OWNERS/OFFICERS/EMPLOYEES

The ATC will not approve any agent whose primary purpose is to handle the transportation needs of its owners, officers or employees, or those of any firm or person having a financial or controlling interest in the agency. Additionally, you should be aware that ATC rules and the Federal Aviation Act of 1958 specifically prohibit an agent from taking a commission for the sale of any air passenger transportation to such persons or entities.

FINANCIAL REQUIREMENTS

Although the Air Traffic Conference does not have any minimum financial standards, an up-to-date financial statement and a minimum $10,000 surety bond which guarantees payments to the airlines is required (the bond must be increased as sales increase). Many travel agents fail every year, generally due to insufficient working capital, over-extension of credit, or lack of management expertise. The failure rate in any small retail business is high and we would suggest that you survey your potential carefully before pursuing this further. Additionally, since the vast majority of newly approved travel agents rarely realize a profit and often times operate under deficit conditions for the first few years of operation, the prospective agent should have an available working capital of at least $25,000 to defray the initial expenses of becoming "established". In fact, you should be prepared to take very little or nothing out of the business by way of personal remuneration at the outset.

ATC APPROVAL

Once approved, the ATC agent has the responsibility to adhere to the terms of the ATC Sales Agency Agreement. Agents are expected by the very terms of the Agreement, not only to maintain the highest business, ethical and professional standards, but also to transact a sufficient amount of business to warrant their continued inclusion on the ATC Agency List of approved agents. One year after approval, the ATC agent may be eligible for reduced rate transportation privileges. You should note, however, that such reduced rate is applicable only to those persons who devote their full-time to the sale and promotion of passenger transportation. Reduced rate will not be granted to absentee owners (i.e.,

EXHIBIT 2 (Page 5)

those who do not devote their full time to the operation of the agency), spouses of owners or employees, or those persons employed in a clerical, secretarial or bookkeeping capacity. These privileges are intended for full-time <u>sales</u> people only.

At present, there are no federal requirements for travel agent or agency licensing. Several States, however, do have licensing requirements and some others have proposed legislation which may become effective at any time. Be sure to check with the appropriate government office in your State.

<u>A BRIEF CHECK LIST</u>

Although the travel agency business is exciting and dynamic, it is also demanding and challenging. You may increase your chances of success, and avoid disillusionment or outright failure, by using the following "check list" before deciding to open an agency.

1. Critically analyze your business and managerial abilities. Remember, a travel agency owner or manager should be a businessman first, a travel lover second.

2. Critically analyze your technical skills or experience, or those of the person you have hired to perform these duties. These skills include familiarity with fare construction, ticketing, Conference reporting, use of industry guides and tariffs, as well as the ability to plan and secure accommodations, sightseeing tours, cruises, etc. properly. And don't forget this person has to have the ability to sell these services to the public.

3. Conduct a careful research of your market potential. Don't assume that you'll simply open your doors and everyone will come running. Begin by determining the nature and volume of your competitors' business - that of the established, experienced agencies in your area. Then determine if and how you can generate <u>new</u> business. If your operation will be based sole<u>ly</u> on the idea of taking business away from existing agencies, your chances of success will be greatly diminished.

The foregoing observations are offered for your benefit, to provide you with a realistic understanding of the travel agency business. Needless to say, there is always a place for the energetic and imaginative professional who sets his goal on being a travel agent. He is the type who would be successful in virtually any business.

If you wish to pursue this matter by filing an application for approval, kindly forward a check in the amount of $10.00 payable to the Air Traffic Conference, along with your specific request and mailing instructions, and we shall be pleased to forward the necessary papers. Please do not send cash.

Travel Agency Administration
AIR TRAFFIC CONFERENCE

EXHIBIT 3

SUGGESTIONS FOR USING THE LIBRARY SYSTEM AND RECORDING NOTES AND INFORMATION

These suggestions are simply my own system worked out over the past few years when I've had to research and study a variety of topics, and offered to those who have not had occasion to do this kind of work before. If you have a better system of your own, by all means use it.

1. First, find out the full range of library services to which you have access:

    a. Does your library card entitle you to use other libraries than the local one?
    b. Does your local library have an inter-library loan system whereby books can be ordered for you?
    c. Ask the librarian for information on special collections that libraries in the area have which might pertain to the topic you are researching.
    d. A polite call to nearby colleges may make it possible for you to use their facilities on a limited basis. Ask for the librarian, rather than directing your request to the first person who answers the phone.

2. Always have notetaking supplies with you when you're on a serious search for information—pens or pencils, a looseleaf notebook, 3x5 cards.

3. Have a basic outline of the information you are seeking and a system to record it:

    a. At the front of the notebook I reserve a few pages to list each book or other information source, numerically. This then is kept there permanently as an index. For instance, if the first book I found on the subject dealt with in this Manual were the SBA book on small business ownership, that would be listed as number 1. The next book would be coded as number 2, and so on.

    b. Then make a list of the subject headings you'll use and assign one or more pages of your notebook to each, with a tab for main headings so that the place can be easily found. For instance for this project I would have a tab for Introduction, plus each Phase, and additional pages for each marginal heading for which you are compiling notes.

    c. When you take notes, code them properly and enter them directly into the notebook in the proper place. For instance if *Dealer in Dreams* were book number 3 and you wanted to note that it contains a very good filing system for travel brochures on page 43, you would simply enter "3/43" on the page of your notebook under Phase Four headed "A Filing System".

EXHIBIT 3, continued

If you did not own this book, or it had been very troublesome and inconvenient to borrow from the library, you might want to record the information itself, rather than indicating where it could be found. In this case, you would have to list all the details, or make a photocopy of page 43 for your files.

4. In some instances two other devices should be used for keeping information:

   a. 3x5 cards and a file box for addresses, telephone numbers, company names, etc. generally anything that is best filed alphabetically.

   b. A set of file folders in which to store bulky information—price lists, catalogs, brochures, applications, etc.

   The cards and folders should be tabbed with basically the same subject headings as your notebook, with sub-heads added whenever warranted.

5. Do a little browsing in the books located near those you've found that are listed in Appendix A. That list contains books with which I am familiar, but your library may have many others that may appeal to you more. Also check out that Dewey Decimal number on the spine of the book on the reference shelves, new book shelves, and oversized book shelves.

6. Always check the bibliography of books you read for leads to other books which may be of interest.

7. Make friends with the librarian or reference librarian and explain what your search is about. A good librarian can direct you to special collections that may be of help to you, government offices and people who might have information you can use, pamphlets and newspaper clippings, etc. kept in the reference room "vertical" files. In our area, for instance, a few libraries have Federal grants to support a special room containing all kinds of materials on vocational guidance, careers, etc. Such a collection might well stock the books listed in Appendix A.

8. Finally, one item you can't get at the library, and is a must. Buy one of the daily record books stationery stores carry for recording appointments, things to do, mileage, lunches, miscellaneous expenses—you need to keep track of this when it comes time to be reimbursed from business funds for out-of-pocket expenses, as well as for your income tax returns.

Phase Two

Legal/Financial Matters

Most of the actual work in Phase Two has to be done by your lawyer and accountant. You, of course, have to participate, to orient yourself, provide them with much financial and personal information, attend meetings, listen, learn, and ultimately make decisions.

Becoming thoroughly familiar with the Conference applications should also be started in this Phase.

Conference Application Kits

The ATC and IATA application kits consist of many pages of forms, instructions, enclosures, etc. When they arrive, make a separate file for each and list each item you've received. Whenever some part of the applications must be removed from the file, for whatever reason, make it a practice to note what has been removed and who has it. Otherwise you may find, by the time you're ready to send in the applications (many months away) that some key page is missing.

Check each application against Appendix C, noting any differences. Obviously you must adjust your procedures to conform to the applications you receive if they differ in any way from this manual.

Make copies of the IATA questionnaire and the ATC application to use as a rough draft. Then you can keep the originals safely filed away until it is time to have them typed up.

Make extra copies of the financial statement forms—the accountant and lawyer will need them.

Understand Their Contents

Read and understand everything in both application kits. Not all at one sitting, of course. But as the agency owner you do have to know basically what they are all about. Much of it is legalese, so knowing what it means is not all that easy. At times you'll need your lawyer to interpret passages for you. If you are new to the industry and plan to have a hired ERP you may have to wait until that individual is hired and can explain the implications of some parts of the sales agreements.

Executing the Agency Sales Agreements is the same as executing any legal contract. As such, they require the understanding and care required for a legal contract. In addition to the rules and regulations outlined in the application kits, the agreements bind you to innumerable other rules and regulations incorporated in Conference resolutions, references, amendments, etc.

Keeping abreast of all these rules and regulations is one of the major responsibilities of your ERP. Nevertheless, you, as owner, are the one held legally responsible for adhering to them. So it behooves you to begin immediately to learn as much as you can about the extent of your commitments when you sign the sales agreements. Once your agency is in operation and your appointments have been received there are seminars and opportunities for training available to you.

Interpreting Conference Requirements

There's little left to interpretation regarding the financial and bonding requirements. Some of the other requirements are not stated as specifically.

Except for a few prohibitions against locating your agency in a hotel or airport, or as part of your residence, there are no minimum size requirements stated. However, Aryear Gregory, mentions that agencies have been turned down for being too small and suggests minimum guidelines that allow for two sales desks with seating space for two customers at each desk, plus a reception area, five filing cabinets, a safe, and extra storage space.

As part of your Conference applications, you must provide photographs and IATA asks for a detailed physical description of the premises. The inspectors who visit your office will definitely be looking for any discrepancies between what you claim and what exists.

Although theoretically the experience requirements can be met by one person, there is a tacit assumption you will have at least two people on your staff. (If you are a newcomer to the industry you probably should hire two people with experience—for a total of three, minimum, counting you.) Practically speaking, it is impossible to maintain normal business hours with just one staff member. Someone must be available to run to the bank, the post office, the airport.

As to sales operations, nothing is spelled out too specifically but inspectors will look for a well-filled brochure rack, the standard travel references, and the appurtenances of a travel agency which is as IATA puts it "...open and readily accessible to the public for (general travel services) and is to be clearly identifiable as a place of business for the sale of passenger transportation and services related thereto."

Only IATA specifically expects proof of your ability to promote the sale of travel. They require evidence of a continuing promotional program and one which emphasizes international air transportation on IATA member airlines.

Hire Your Lawyer and Accountant

If you haven't already done so, now is the time when you must decide on and hire a lawyer and an accountant.

The legal and financial aspects of starting a business seem the most intimidating and complicated. Yet, if you allow sufficient time for the necessary meetings, the legal and financial problems should present the least difficulty simply because this is one area where you will be able to have the experts take care of most of the work.

But you do need to allow enough time. It takes time to even come up with the right questions. Good lawyers and accountants are busy, so that sometimes you can't schedule meetings as quickly as you'd like. Don't be tempted, however, to gloss over details because you're impatient to get on with looking for a location and getting started.

And expect a few hassles and difficult times during Phase Two. A lovely, spontaneous idea to open a travel agency comes up against the hard realities of making financial commitments, working out a partnership agreement perhaps, and sometimes hearing some very pessimistic advice.

Working With Experts

Your lawyer and accountant are the first in a series of experts you'll be working with. This is a good point to offer a few personal observations on how best to work with an expert. Whether lawyer, accountant, or the caterer for your Open House, these suggestions apply:

- Have an agenda for every meeting, even if it's only a few scribbled notes on a scrap of paper. Try to pace the meeting so you get through the entire agenda. Try not to get off on a tangent and end up going home without ever reaching the last few items.
- Learn the terminology before you go. Don't show up, for example, at a lawyer's office to plan a partnership agreement, without first having reviewed what you've read on the subject, and are familiar with some of the terms you need to know.
- If you have a partner, make it an inflexible rule to discuss items on the agenda BEFORE you get to your meeting. If some new item crops up during the session don't be rushed into any decision on it until you've had time to think it over alone.
- Find out the best time to call your expert, how long it takes to get an appointment. To some degree, you must pace your progress on the workload and working hours of your experts.
- Again, as for any meetings with your partner or staff, make written notes on what has been decided and/or discussed. This is even a good idea for telephone calls. If you don't, inevitably there will be disagreements or delays later because participants have varying recollections of what was said or agreed.

Choosing a Legal Structure for the Agency

Sole ownership is simplest. If a partner, or partners, is involved, things become far more complicated. In either case, the decision as to whether or not you'll incorporate is one of those critical decisions, deserving the utmost care.

Travel agencies are increasingly plagued with law suits, or the threat of law suits. Errors and Omissions insurance may not be available to you as a brand new agency. Get clarification on this point. Also, read one or more of the books listed in Appendix A on the whole question of travel agencies and the law. Ask your lawyer to look them over too, if he is not experienced in representing travel agencies.

You can't make an intelligent decision on whether or not to incorporate without these precautions.

Partners and Partnerships

If yours is to be a partnership (whether incorporated or not), there are things to consider both on a personal level and a financial level, before making a final commitment. There are both advantages and disadvantages in having someone to share in the financing and responsibilities of the agency.

Probably you should be as fussy and demanding about the partner you choose as the staff you hire. In reality, however, partnerships seem to be put together on the same basis as many marriages—propinquity and impulse.

You can probably think of many more personal and personality factors that would be important to you. Here's just a few factors I believe are important to consider in choosing a partner:

- Relative financial positions—comparable, or will one of you be less able to take risks?
- Too great a disparity in ages, family responsibilities?
- Goals and future plans for the agency; will one of you want to sell out long before the other?
- What's your lawyer's and accountant's opinion of the two (or three, or more) of you as a viable partnership?
- Are your travel industry or general business experience and skills complementary?
- Do you agree on a basic philosophy for running the agency as to specialization, general image, marketing and sales ideas, fam trips, outside sales reps or not, and so on?
- Then there are the petty things that can escalate into major sources of irritation—nepotism (how do each of you feel about hiring friends or family), division of responsibility for the tedious chores, habitual tardiness or absenteeism, smoking or not smoking, tolerance for clutter, etc., etc.

I suppose, like a marriage, if you waited for the perfect partner, you'd never get going at all. I just want to emphasize that a business partnership is a personal relationship, as well as a financial and legal entity, and personal factors must be considered.

If you've selected a lawyer and accountant experienced in handling small business accounts, listen to what they have to say on the subject.

A Partner as the ERP

If you, or one of your partners, is also the ERP and will provide the experience asked for by the Conferences, now is the time to make sure this experience can be substantiated by the necessary letters of reference.

If you are providing only financial backing for the venture and relying on a partner to fulfill ERP role, and this individual is not well known to you personally, you need to exercise the same caution in checking out his or her references as you would for a hired ERP.

The Partnership Agreement

The terms of your partnership agreement is something you must rely on your lawyer to handle properly. He will know what the agreement (or incorporation terms) should include based on his experience and the particular circumstances.

However, there's one item, peculiar to travel agencies, that deserves special attention. And that is the establishment of a dollar value on the business at any point in its life.

Obviously, there must be provisions detailing what happens if one of you should die, become incapacitated, or just want out. The usual guidelines your accountant and lawyer suggest may not be wise or suitable for a travel agency. Why? Because there seems to be no set of guidelines accepted industry-wide for dealing with this question.

To make my point, I've included as Exhibit 5, a summary of a recent law suit in New Jersey involving the Hillsdale Travel Agency, as described in a news item in the trade press. You will see that the various experts called on to help the court decide what the agency was worth gave opinions ranging from zero to $102,000!

So be forewarned and insist that your legal agreements state exactly how value will be determined, and understand what that means in specific dollars and cents.

A Name and a Logo

Chronologically, this item could be placed in a couple of spots, depending on your idea of a good name for your agency.

If the name is to be based on your name, or your partner's name, or is one of those manufactured names combining a couple of personal names, than you can make your choice early in the whole process and begin work on a logo and a letterhead design.

If you prefer something keyed to travel—The Travel Desk, or Travelin' Man, or some such—you will have to check to see that it hasn't already been taken by another travel agency in your area.

If you want an agency name that reflects its location or the type of premises you're looking for, then choosing it just will have to wait for that signed lease.

Whatever your choice, be prepared with some tentative ideas for a logo and letterhead and how the artwork will be done.

Financial Commitments and a Working Budget

You, and any partners involved, will have to provide your lawyer and accountant with personal financial information from which they can prepare the bond application, financial statements for the Conferences, partnership or incorporation agreements. Finalizing some of these documents may have to await your choice of a location, but at this point you need to be assured that you do have the capital you need and that your partners can produce the amounts of money agreed on.

Before going further, prepare a working budget for pre-opening day expenses and for the first year or so after you open. It can help you to keep from spending too much on some aspect of the agency, to the detriment of something else.

You can use Exhibit 6, or you can devise your own set of categories or one your accountant suggests. Add to these figures the working capital which must be maintained and the net worth which must be documented. Then there is the question of salaries for you and any partners, or an allowance for living expenses.

After it's all put together you should know, with your accountant's advice, whether you have the necessary capital to carry you through the first couple of years. You can also decide or at least discuss how additional capital will be raised if it is needed.

Winding Up Phase Two Your lawyer and accountant may want to wait to prepare some of the documents until you have a location and an address. However all the discussion and working drafts of the financial statements, partnership agreement, incorporation should be completed before you begin the actual search for a location and any staff you plan to hire.

Don't get impatient with this process. It can take far more time than you expected until all details are properly worked out to the satisfaction of all having a financial interest in the business. Then there are delays because you can't always get appointments as quickly as you'd prefer with the lawyer and accountant.

In the coming weeks you will keep in touch with the progress of the legal/financial work involved, as occasion warrants. Be sure that the bond application and the request for a Federal employment number are filed at the earliest possible moment. Then check a few weeks later and regularly thereafter, to be sure they are in hand by the time you must submit your Conference applications.

Start a Draft of the Applications Speaking of these applications—you can begin working on the rough draft on that extra copy you made, whenever you have the necessary information for a particular answer. If you work on the applications a bit at a time they won't be such a tedious task at the end.

EXHIBIT 4

CHECKLIST FOR ESTIMATING CAPITAL REQUIREMENTS

Typical Rental for Office Space
    Major shopping malls
    Medium-sized malls with supermarket
    Shopping "strip" centers
    Specialty areas, boutiques
    Unconventional possibilities
    Location in center of town
    Houses on fringe of business area
    Office buildings—ground and upper floor locations

Utility Costs—Installation, Rates, Deposits
    Telephone
    Heat
    Electricity
    Air Conditioning
    Garbage and rubbish removal
    Snow removal
    General maintenance

Legal/Accounting/Financial
    Start-up and retainer legal fees
    One-time and continuing costs for partnership or incorporation
    General insurance: fire, theft, etc.
    Errors and omissions insurance
    Start-up and retainer accounting fees
    Maintenance of bond
    Conference application fees and annual membership: ATC, IATA, IPSA, TPPC, AMTRAK
    Interest costs if you plan to borrow $15,000 working capital, $20,000 net worth requirements
    How does your available capital measure up to guidelines in Exhibit 2?

Staffing (Personnel)
    Typical salary and fringe benefits for an ERP
    Typical salary and fringe benefits for other staff you will hire
    Social Security and other payroll costs for employees

Advertising and Promotion
    Yellowpages ads of various sizes
    Local newspaper ad space art
    Direct mail: addressing and stuffing envelopes, collating, postage rates, bulk rates
    Printing: offset, typesetting, artwork
    Rates and costs for any other media you plan to use

Travel Supplies and References
    Office forms
    Reference Books
    Trade magazine subscriptions
    Travel Guides

Office Supplies and Equipment
    Stationery and general office supplies
    Desk accessories
    New and used desks and chairs
    New and used file cabinets and office furniture
    Reception area furniture
    New and used typewriters
    Adding machines, calculators
    A safe; a locked file cabinet

EXHIBIT 5

WHAT IS A TRAVEL AGENCY WORTH?

Specifically—when the owners of an established agency, grossing $1,000,000 in annual sales, decide to split, how much should Owner A (remaining owner) pay to Owner B (departing owner)?

In a recent court case in New Jersey, as reported by Travel Weekly, expert opinions ranged from minus (less than zero) to $102,000! Here's a summary of how this interesting situation developed.

Being unable to arrive at an amicable agreement, and, I assume, there being no partnership agreement covering this point, the Hillsdale Travel case ended up in litigation, with owner B suing Owner A for satisfactory settlement.

At the first hearing, two non-travel industry experts testified that the agency had a minus value. The judge thought this was "ridiculous" and "of no help" and set his own value of $50,000 ($39,000 plus $11,000 for good will). Thus Owner A was to pay Owner B $25,000 for her share of the agency.

Owner A appealed the decision. In the next go-round, two experts with travel industry background were called. But their opinions varied greatly with one setting a value of $7,500 and the other $48,000. Owner B then brought in a third expert from the travel industry who said the agency's value was between $68,000 and $102,000 and outlined a series of variables that would apply in determining a low or high valuation within this range.

In the end the judge arrived at a decision very similar to that of the original judge, ordering Owner A to pay Owner B the sum of $24,000.

The article then closes with this: "Attorneys observing the case said that agency partners may be able to avoid litigation if they prepare a shareholders agreement before starting up. Such an agreement should stipulate how an agency's value will be determined if one of the partners decides to sell or if there is a need to determine the firm's value for some other reason. The agreement could also include a provision that would give a partner less money for his share of the business if he decided to re-enter the agency business within a certain period of time or within a nearby area."

As a new agency owner, what can you learn from all this and what criteria can you use to include a clause in your partnership agreement that could avoid costly and acrimonious litigation on this point?

First, to again quote from Travel Weekly: "Professional appraisers, brokers, or lawyers without an acquaintance with the (travel) field are of little use." And the first expert opinion which gave Hillsdale Travel a value of minus, or zero, seems to bear this out. Therefore, this is one area which you and any partners must come up with a formula that satisfies all concerned even if it runs counter to what your lawyer suggests. The facts above indicate that the typical formulas used by lawyers and accountants for evaluating service-type businesses do not necessarily apply to travel agencies.

Second, the formulas mentioned in the articles are all based on 2-3 years' of sales records. Therefore, as a new agency owner, your partnership or incorporation agreements must also include a method of determining value until the agency has been established for a period of time.

Third, here are a few formulas mentioned in the articles which you can consider and the reading you do from Appendix A may suggest a few more:

      4-14% of gross sales

      $5,000 for every $100,000 of gross sales

      70-130% of average annual gross commissions for last 2-3 years

      5% of gross sales at 8.5% commission, with $10,000 more for average commission sales for each 1/10th of 1% above 8.5; you would subtract $5,000 for each 1/10th of 1% below 8.5

      2-3 times average net profit over three years

      6 times net earnings, after taxes, based on past three years

All seem to agree that factors such as type of business, reputation of the agency, transferability of clients to new owners, mix of commercial/pleasure commissions, etc., were factors to consider in determining whether an agency should be valued at the low or high side of the formula used.

The court settlement in the Hillsdale case was finally based on a formula suggested by ASTA based on gross commissions earned over most recent three years, but providing a range that takes into account the many variables that determine the quality of an agency operation. The judge chose the low end of the range, adjudging the agency as being worth, $82,317, which figure he then further adjusted because of loss of goodwill, disruption of the business by loss of a partner, cash assets and "other complicating factors."

EXHIBIT 6

CHECKLIST FOR PLANNING A WORKING BUDGET

Start-up and One-Time Costs

Legal start-up fees
Accounting start-up fees
Remodeling, redecorating of office
Furnishings and equipment
Reception area
Safe and/or locked file cabinet
Installation of utilities
Promotion and advertising for opening
Conference appointment fees
Miscellaneous one-time expenditures

Add to this, the amount for rental and utility deposits—not spent money, but not yours to use either.

Monthly/Annual Costs for Maintaining the Agency

Salaries for employees and benefits
Interest on borrowed capital
Rent (or other premises-ownership costs)
Utilities and maintenance of premises
Legal and accounting fees
Insurance of all kinds
Maintaining your bond
Annual Conference fees
General office supplies
Travel forms and supplies
Travel reference books and subscriptions
   (incl. trade magazines)
Postage
Education: Fam trips, seminars, travel education
   courses and transportation
Advertising and promotion
Miscellaneous

Add to your figures an amount for owner salaries and/or loss of income you would otherwise be earning, or whatever computation your accountant suggests in order to understand realistically what the agency is costing you until it turns a profit.

Maintenance of the $20,000 minimum net worth and $15,000 in working capital, is a continuing Conference requirement.

Phase Three

Premises and Personnel

The search for a location and an ERP (if you need to hire one) is roughly concurrent. If you, or a partner, is providing the experience needed to satisfy Conference requirements, then Phase Three becomes far simpler. If you must hire an ERP, then ideally you should know who this key person is going to be by the time you sign your lease, at the latest.

The steps involved in finding a location and an ERP, are basically the same, even though one is a place-search and the other a people-search:
- Determine standards, specifications, qualifications, conditions you are seeking
- Decide on the techniques you'll use to find them
- The search itself—inspecting, making inquiries, interviewing, checking references, etc.
- Making the final decision and having your lawyer take care of whatever legalities are involved

Once you have a signed lease, or other proof of ownership of office space, and thus an address, you can begin work on Phase Four while finishing up Phase Three.

Specifications for Premises and Personnel

The experts seem to agree that just about every business decision you make in establishing your agency, begins with the clientele you hope to reach. Where do you expect your customers to come from? This is the key factor in determining location, the kind of staff you need, the promotion and advertising you do. It is all interrelated.

So before you even begin to draw up a list of specifications for your office space and the ERP, begin by considering the markets you want to reach. Economic and social status, travel habits, age groups, level of income and disposable income, ethnic considerations, all are part of a marketing approach.

Also—do you have any plans to seek out and serve groups or special interest travelers, or will you rely on walk-in business? Do you anticipate a large following from social and business contacts you already have? Do you plan to look for commercial clients as well as vacation travelers?

With all these considerations in mind, use the checklists in Exhibits 7 and 8 to draw up a picture of the ideal location and staff you hope to find.

Techniques for Finding Them

You probably will check the classified real estate columns of local newspapers or advertise in them yourself, in looking for office space. Or you can turn it over to a real estate broker who specializes in business space.

To begin with, however, simply driving up and down each street in the general area you are considering is a good idea. It's the only way also of knowing where your competition is. As you drive around you can stop and speak to business owners, building and shopping center managers, to ask about present and future vacancies. If you find a building that interests you but is totally vacant, you can call the local tax office to find out who owns it.

As to staff, within the industry it seems that word-of-mouth recommendations and personal contacts are the most common hiring method. However, if you must hire an ERP you probably don't have these industry contacts. Your best bet is to place a help wanted ad in local newspapers and/or the trade press. The trade magazines often carry ads also of people looking for jobs.

If you are writing a help wanted ad, avoid using a box number unless there is some special reason you must do so. You may miss out on some good candidates who are afraid to answer a blind ad for fear it may turn out to be their own boss, or a friend of the boss. Try to give enough identifying information so that a candidate can respond without revealing his or her identity.

There are agencies specializing in travel agency jobs but these are only in major cities. Still, they may have knowledge of possible candidates in your area.

Deciding on a Location

Choosing a location is, in my opinion, the riskiest of all the decisions you have to make, simply because it is so difficult and costly to correct, if you've made a poor decision. You are usually bound to a costly lease. If you've spent money on remodeling and redecorating, that money cannot be recovered should you wish to move elsewhere. And, in fact, you may not be able to get out of the lease at all.

There's all kinds of information to be had from local planning boards about income levels, population and growth trends, business forecasts, economic potentials of an area. However, it takes a degree of sophisticated business knowledge to evaluate the information. If you're a first-time small business owner, much of this information and statistics may be over your head.

The books listed in Appendix A have much to say about how to choose a good location for a business. The Exhibits at the end of this Phase can help by reminding you of some of the many points to consider.

You also may be able to get some good advice from local business people or bank officers, or the local office of the SBA. And, of course, you can call on a travel management consultant to second guess your judgment after you've narrowed down the possibilities.

Minimum Staffing Requirements

The Conferences mandate that you have at least one person, meeting both qualifications described, working full time in your agency by opening day. The implications of this requirement vary, according to the situation you're in, which will generally be one of the three listed below. Depending on whether you fall into category 1, 2, or 3, following are the minimum staff you'll need. Obviously you can have more staff than this if you wish.

1) Yours is a joint or group endeavor with two or more persons having a financial interest, and one or more of you can meet the ERP requirements. In this case you really don't have to hire anyone at all at the beginning.

2) Your venture is a sole proprietorship, or a partnership, but none of the owners qualifies as the ERP. You definitely must hire at least one person to fulfill ERP qualifications. And, in fact, Mr. Gregory says that unofficially IATA expects travel agency owners with no industry experience to have two qualified employees, even though it is not mentioned in the IATA application instructions.

3) Yours is a sole proprietorship and you also meet all the experience requirements. You still need at least one employee (or a combination of part-timers) but that employee need not necessarily be a travel agent. You need an extra body to run errands, pick up tickets, and so on, since you, as the ERP must remain in the agency virtually every hour it is open as stated on your application forms.

Importance of the ERP You Choose Every step of the hiring process, from defining qualifications to the actual hiring, is far more critical if you are in category 2 and have no industry experience at all as owner(s). The ERP you must hire not only has to earn your appointments but must be relied on to get the business off the ground as well. The hiring decisions you have to make, therefore, have far more serious implications than for those in categories 1 or 3.

I believe it used to be quite common, and I know of a couple of instances myself, where inexperienced new owners would hire someone with two years' experience just long enough to earn their appointments and then let that person go. Apart from the wisdom of doing this, I don't see how it would be possible to get away with it under current regulations since you must keep the Conferences informed of any changes in personnel involving the individual or individuals whose employment earned you your appointments.

The two years' experience is really minimal and you will find in your reading that the experts recommend hiring the best person you can afford, with a minimum of five years' experience. Also, there has been a distinct shift in emphasis in the instructions from the Conferences as of this year. The promotional experience requirement cannot be met by two years' experience as a travel agent who handles walk-in customers, or already established accounts.

Whether you are to function as your own ERP, or this person is to be hired, rereadPar. 1, under Personnel Qualifications, of the ATC document in Exhibit 2.

Certainly if you fall into category 2, you should also do some extra reading on the subject of hiring and evaluating travel agency employees. Mr. Stevens' book, listed in Appendix A is the only one I know of devoted to this topic.

The Lease and Employee Contracts

Once your premises have been found and, if necessary, an ERP hired, your lawyer will again be involved. He will examine the lease and negotiate the best deal possible for you. Also you can call on him to investigate or clarify any local licensing laws, outdoor sign regulations, zoning ordinances, etc., that affect the use of your space.

If you plan to draw up contracts for any employees you hire, the lawyer would probably be involved in that area too. Travel agencies increasingly ask for some commitment on the part of new employees that they will not leave to take employment in an agency located nearby, and to protect the agency's house mailing list from use by departed employees. There is some controversy, however, as to the value of any such commitments or contracts.

A Things-To-Do List

Here's a list of some things to do once you have decided on the office space for your agency, and thus have an address:

1) Put up a large sign, visible from the street, that a new travel agency is about to open. It may just cause that potential future competitor who is stalking the area for office space (just as you were doing up until a few days ago), to look elsewhere.

53

2) Arrange to have theft, fire, liability, and other insurance go into effect as soon as you are legally responsible for the premises.

3) Change the locks and have new keys made. Arrange for installation of any other security devices you feel are necessary, or are necessary to meet Conference requirements.

4) If you haven't already done so, now you simply must choose a name and a logo.

5) Order stationery and business cards.

6) Order the outdoor overhead sign.

7) Make necessary phone calls, deposits, etc. to have utilities installed and turned on; you also need to know your assigned telephone number as soon as possible for printing business cards and stationery.

8) Start attending trade shows, or have your ERP do so, whenever possible to get a headstart on acquiring brochures, and other information you need as part of Phase Four.

Select Your Bank   This item, in some circumstances, could be handled as part of Phase Two. I placed it here, after the acquisition of an address, because proximity to your bank is a factor to consider. Travel agency operations involve daily or twice daily trips to the bank. So it makes sense to choose one near the agency, or on the way home for one of the owners. If you can also manage to have the post office en route to the bank, that's even better since daily trips to the post office is another part of your schedule.

You may wish to use two banks—one for your airline ticketing sales and one for all other business. As you know by now, from reading the application information, you are required to authorize the Area Bank to draw against your business checking account for the amount of your weekly air sales report. Most travel agencies elect to use a separate checking account for this purpose in case of mistakes or computer errors, and some feel that a totally different bank is warranted to protect their general account from being overdrawn through errors by the Area Bank.

Having selected your bank, or banks, following then has to be done:

1) Make a deposit of at least $20,000 in your general account; get a letter from the bank verifying this deposit or have them complete the statement on the reverse side of ATC's financial statement.

2) As you make expenditures from this account, be prepared to deposit additional funds so that a working capital of $15,000 and a net worth of $20,000 can be maintained.

3) Execute the letter in your ATC application kit authorizing the bank in which your ATC checking account is established to honor withdrawals by the Area Bank from this account; ask for two cancelled checks (these will be one of the enclosures you need later for your ATC application).

4) Arrange for a safety deposit box, night drop bag and keys at one or both banks. These are needed to meet ticket security requirements, unless you plan to acquire the special large safe and retain all ticket stock in your office.

5) Have the accountant instruct you in maintaining the checkbooks properly, and reimburse you for any out-of-pocket expenses incurred prior to setting up the checking accounts.

Designing and Decorating the Office

Phase Three ends with your drawing up a detailed plan for transforming the premises acquired into the travel agency you have in mind. The plan should include a list of what needs to be done, who will do it, and a timetable for keeping on top of the whole project so that it is done in time for your tentative opening day. (Use Exhibit 9 as a starting checklist).

You may need to do nothing more than a bit of painting, have the utilities turned on, and move in. At the other end of the scale your premises may require total remodeling and redecorating involving a full range of building contractors.

EXHIBIT 7

CHECKLIST FOR SETTING STANDARDS AND EVALUATING TRAVEL AGENCY PREMISES AND LOCATION

The General Area

Demographic Factors: income, age, social status—marketing questions
Minimum distance from competition
Number of travel agenciess in given radius
Specific towns, areas, streets preferred
Specific towns, areas, streets ruled out
Growing or declining area
Destination area or arterial street
General visual attractiveness
Accessibility by foot, auto, public transportation
Type of space desired—center of town, shopping center, office building, upstairs location, industrial park, house zoned for business, etc.
Desirable adjacent businesses
Undesirable adjacent businesses
Accessibility to banks, post office
Accessibility to agency owners' homes
Average rent in the area

Add any other special qualities or considerations that specifically describe your "ideal" location and premises

Specific Location

Visual attractiveness of immediate area and approach to area
Does building and area appear to be well maintained and managed?
Does the type of customer I want have reason to come to this location, and for what reason?
Could I project the agency image I want at this location?
Will the cost of occupying these premises fall within my working budget?
Are the terms of the lease reasonable and typical as to length, renewal options, sublet privileges, services, maintenance costs, etc. ?
What unfavorable limitations are built into the lease?
What local ordinances, or lease provisions, are there to protect me from undesirable types of business, displays, signs, etc. by the landlord or other nearby tenants?
What does the lawyer think of the lease?

EXHIBIT 7, continued

Specific Office Space

Could these premises be occupied as is? If not, do they require redecorating, reconstruction work, or both?

Do the dimensions meet my minimum guidelines?
Is there possibility for expansion, if needed?
Does the space lend itself to a good agency layout with a logical place for the desks I need, a counter (if planned), brochure racks, storage area, reception area, lavatory, etc.?
What about the window display area as to size, usability, and visibility?
(Draw a diagram to scale of the space, make cutouts of desks and other furniture you plan to use to see what kind of layouts are possible)

What work needs doing on the exterior, in order to make it visible and attractive?
What kind of an overhead sign is possible?
What limitations are there as to signs, installation of awnings, displays, etc., that I must adhere to?

Does this space meet my standards for accessibility by foot, car, public transportation?
Is it easily visible from the street? By drivers of passing cars?
Are the speed limits favorable? Is the parking area an easy turn-off for cars?
Is there sufficient parking space and is it well maintained?

After thorough evaluation, get preliminary estimates for the work needed to make this space into the kind of travel agency you have in mind. Will these make-ready costs fit into your working budget?

Talk to the other tenants and to nearby business owners. What do they think of the area, the landlord, the potential for a travel agency here?

Finally, look into the history of this location. Has it been successful or has there been a high turnover? This is a factor repeated over and over again in books I read on choosing a business location. In one way or another, they made the point that if a location has a history of failed businesses, there may be "subtle factors, not immediately identifiable, at work" and that an unsuccessful environment is almost impossible to overcome. The reason being that each business in an unsuccessful area "must establish its own momentum instead of feeding off the success of other businesses located nearby."

Try to answer these questions:
Would this space benefit from an image of success projected by other businesses located nearby?
What seems to be the combined influence of already established businesses and would a travel agency be an appropriate addition?

EXHIBIT 8

CHECKLIST FOR SETTING STANDARDS, INTERVIEWING, HIRING OF STAFF AND FOR DEVISING AN APPLICATION FORM

Personal Data	Name, address, telephone number, Social Security number, marital status. Is applicant bonded or bondable, can credit references be checked?
Education	Degrees and courses at high school, college, other Travel courses, seminars, fam trips, etc.
Work History	Present employer, can he be contacted? Reason for leaving, length of time worked, duties, responsibilities, salary.
	Same information for prior employment.
Travel Industry Experience	Specific travel experience in jobs listed: types of travel (group, FIT, airline ticketing, cruises, commercial, etc.); commissions record, "following", etc.
Contacts	Clubs, avocations, business and social connections from which travel sales might develop
Travel Knowledge	Countries and cities visited, areas of the U.S., whether as a travel agent, resident, or visited on a personal pleasure trip. Fam trips taken.
Personal Qualities	Appearance, voice, manner, smoker or not—any purely personal attribute that is important to you
Special Skills To Offer	Typing, other office machines; bookkeeping experience; languages; writing, advertising or sales promotion skills, window displays, etc.
Meeting Conference Requirements (if necessary)	Airline ticketing and/or sales promotional experience—do letters of reference and a personal check of former employers support experience claimed?
	Are responses to Conference application questions concerning personnel satisfactory? What is reputation for integrity of former employers?

EXHIBIT 8, continued

These are points to check on your total staffing situation, which are not specifically accounted for in the Conference staffing requirements. Yet, they are essential to the total job of running an agency.

If you, your partner, or staff members, are weak in any of these areas, plans should be made for someone acquiring the necessary experience and training to fill the gap.

1) Know enough about Conference and industry rules and regulations to avoid violation of the Agency Sales Agreements regarding ticketing, fares, reservations, security of ticket stock, sales reports, reduced rate travel, etc.

2) Thorough knowledge of the references, interpreting brochures, using travel agency forms and procedures and a continuing system for keeping up with new information that comes into the agency each day.

3) Sufficient experience to properly evaluate the integrity and quality of tour company offerings, as well as other wholesalers and suppliers.

4) Willingness to participate in local and national trade organizations, training seminars, trade shows, etc.

5) Have contacts in the industry to help smooth problems that arise.

6) The ability to communicate and train other staff (perhaps even you) in travel sales and ticketing; ability to retain and inspire loyalty in staff.

7) Familiarity with bookkeeping system used; a basic understanding of accounting terminology, cash flow problems, cost analysis of various travel agency operations.

8) Creativity and open-mindedness in exploring new products, approaches, marketing ideas in an industry that is increasingly competitive and demanding.

EXHIBIT 9

CHECKLIST FOR REMODELING AND/OR REDECORATING OFFICE SPACE

Major Remodeling
    Adequate wiring and electrical outlets
    Lighting
    Ceilings, walls
    Floors and surface covering
    Additional partitions
    A counter
    Reception area
    Storage area, shelving
    Bathroom facilities
    Area for preparing and storing and beverages

Floor Plan
    Sales desks and chairs
    Customer chairs
    Brochure racks
    Typing tables
    File cabinets
    Locked file cabinet and/or safe
    Storage and work area for ticket stock, validator, plates
    Coat racks for staff and clients
    Reception area
    Counter

Color Scheme
    Major surfaces: ceilings, walls, floors, trim
    Accent colors
    Upholstery, chair coverings
    Draperies, window treatment
    Outdoor awnings, or other outdoor color use

Accessories
    Plants
    Travel posters
    Travel accessories
    Accessories for each sales station and desk

Equipment
    Typewriters, outlets and lighting for them
    Adding Machine, calculators
    Bookkeeping records area
    Travel reference shelves for references used by all
    Travel library
    Equipment used for mailings

Outdoor Sign—Exterior Changes

Listing in Main Lobby

Window Display, and eye-level sign of agency name and hours

Miscellaneous
    Arrangements for photographs required by Conferences
    Cleaning Supplies
    Bathroom Supplies
    Kitchen area equipment and supplies

Other:_____

_____

Phase Four

Sales: Set-up and Promotion

At this point, the redecorating/remodeling of your office space should be under way, with you keeping tabs on everything so that it keeps moving forward and will be ready for your tentative opening day. Furniture and equipment have been ordered to arrive at appropriate moments, and arrangements have been made for installation of utilities.

Phase Four involves the dual activity of (1) getting the office ready for operation as a travel agency, and (2) planning and implementing the sales promotion campaign required by IATA.

As in Phase Three, it's best to have written plans and lists of things-to-do, for the various activities.

Get Ready for Travel Sales

Getting the office ready for sales operations involves:
- Notifying the companies and people who ought to know of your new travel agency about to open
- Acquiring the supplies, brochures and reference books that are the stock-in-trade of a travel agency
- Displaying the brochures, posters, 3-dimensional displays that make your office look like a travel agency
- Establishing policies and procedures for a functioning office that can handle travel sales
- Setting up a filing system and bookkeeping system

The over-all planning is a job for you and/or the ERP. Implementing the plans, however, can be assigned to all staff members.

Using Exhibit 10 to help jog your memory, plus a copy of the Travel Industry Personnel Guide, plus any of the travel agency management books you've acquired as part of your reading plan, prepare a series of lists—

- Companies to be contacted for brochures now and to request you be added to their mailing lists
- Reference books and subscriptions to be ordered
- Principals and suppliers to be contacted
- Travel agency forms and supplies needed
- General office supplies needed
- Display materials and racks; supplies to have on hand for creating displays

Note also where and how each item will be acquired—local purchase, phone orders, a form postcard or letter, or individually written letters or order forms.

Then just get started! If you've followed earlier advice you should have catalogs on hand, as well as order forms and current price information on references you need to order. Also, perhaps by this time you and/or your ERP have been able to attend a few trade shows and have picked up some brochures and the company order cards for ordering in the future.

You may want to combine your mailing to some of the principals and suppliers with an announcement card, or an invitation to your open house, just to save postage. Also check with your post office for current requirements that might enable you to do a bulk mailing at lower cost.

Plan a Sales Promotion Campaign

Your sales promotion plan is a job you may have decided to turn over to professionals. If you plan to do it yourself, this decision should have been made early enough to give you time to acquire some of the information and skills needed.

Writing press releases, preparing copy and art work for ads, doing pasteups, preparing camera-ready materials, learning the regulations and requirements for bulk mailings and how to deal with the post office—these skills are all required for even a modest sales promotion plan. The books listed in Appendix A contain much helpful information. Check also the vertical files and card catalog of your local library.

Fortunately, you can also obtain a great deal of help and advice from the staff of the media you use. You'll most certainly use the services of a printer and they too can be of great help. Or, you can make a compromise decision and handle those parts of your sales promotion plan within your capabilities and hire freelancers for those parts that are over your head.

Your sales promotion plan should include—
- The media you'll use
- The message to be conveyed in each ad, or mailing piece, or whatever
- Timing for each part of the plan and the various deadlines involved for each item in the plan
- Who will be responsible for executing each part of your plan—staff members, professionals, print shops, etc.
- Estimated costs for each part, and an overall budget for the entire plan
- Some standards for evaluating the success or failure of each part of the campaign, so you'll know which segments or approaches are worth repeating

IATA Guidelines for Sales Promotion

IATA requires: "Evidence of a continuing promotional programme... (which) includes but is not limited to one or more of the following: (i) advertising related to international air transportation on the services of IATA Member airlines in newspapers and/or other media; (ii) film showings; (iii) production of travel brochures; (iv) direct mail promotion."

So you have a great deal of leeway. The sky's the limit, if you can afford it; or you can devise a plan that meets these criteria that can be quite modest in cost.

Here's what we did, which was evidently satisfactory at that time—
- Bought a medium-sized yellowpages ad
- Ran three pre-opening day ads in each of the two local weekly papers, for the three weeks just before opening day, inviting residents to stop by
- Sent a press release (which was published) to each of the local weeklies giving personal and background information on the agency owners

- Bought three ads in one of those giveaway shoppers' papers that are delivered door-to-door, emphasizing international air travel and package air tours
- Had a thousand formal announcement cards made up which included an invitation to our Open House; this was sent to trade people, local business owners, nearby residents, friends and acquaintances
- Started a weekly ad in the local papers, in the form of a travel "column" featuring timely travel suggestions
- Described our plan for a quarterly newsletter to be sent to a house mailing list; we put this into effect within a couple weeks after opening day so that we could demonstrate a "continuing programme"

Coordination and Deadlines

The one thing, I think, to remember for the amateur attempting to handle his own promotion campaign, is that it requires a great deal of coordination. Also, everthing you do seems to require much more time than you anticipate.

What is involved is a creative process—no matter how modest your effort may be. It takes time to write a well-organized and interesting news release. It takes time to devise even the simplest ad to be sure it says what you want it to say, covers all the essentials, reads well and looks good.

Be sure you are aware of all the deadlines involved and to have them noted on your calendar; be sure to allow for holidays when deadlines have a way of being shortened. Be sure your ERP checks each segment of your plan to make certain you are not violating any Conference regulations in your text, promises, prices, etc.

Finally, be sure to keep copies of every ad, news release, flier, or mailing piece. One set must be submitted with your IATA application and you should have extras on hand for visiting inspectors. Since IATA specifically uses the word "continuing" in its instructions, you should also retain copies of items which are part of your publicity campaign after the application has been submitted.

Do the creative planning for your promotion activities well ahead of time if this aspect of the business worries you. Then, if you sense any part of it is beyond your capabilities, there's still time to hire help, rather than waste your promotional budget on a poorly executed campaign.

Agency Policies and Procedures

You may not wish to prepare a full-fledged policies and procedures manual before opening day, but you will certainly need to have discussed and settled on a system for handling client phone calls, walk-ins, general inquiries, as well as individual travel counseling. You also need a system for making the reservations, invoicing, preparing vouchers, receipts—the paperwork involved in implementing sales.

Another immediate task is a system for handling incoming mail and brochures as well as a policy and system for stamping, filing, and circulating brochures and other sales materials so that each staff member is assured of keeping up with the information.

Working hours must be established and posted on the front door and/or window. This information is included in your applications so it must be a schedule that can be adequately handled by the staff available.

Air Travel Sales

Particular attention must be paid to handling air travel sales between opening day and when your Conference appointments are received. The ERP should contact each airline rep individually and ask how each wishes to have air sales handled and ticketed during this interim period, as well as any special instructions for recording and collecting commissions.

We found some airlines more accommodating than others. One international airline insisted on a certified check accompanying each request for tickets, yet another was quite willing to send the tickets to the agency by mail if time permitted. One of the domestic airlines was extremely helpful in agreeing to write any domestic ticket for us at a nearby local airport, so that only international tickets had to be picked up at a much more distant major airport.

I've heard of commission-splitting arrangements that some new agencies make with nearby established agencies, but to my knowledge this is really against all regulations. Also, I don't see how the unapproved agency could build up any record of travel sales using this system.

Eventually, once appointed, you will receive all the commissions you're entitled to for air sales, if you've kept proper records and filed the necessary forms.

**Set Up
A Filing
System**

Try to have your filing cabinets installed, and a filing system set up and ready to go before the deluge of mail starts to arrive.

A minimum of three or four letter-sized files, plus one legal-sized cabinet fitted with dividers to accommodate hotel brochures should be adequate for a start. At least one cabinet needs a lock to meet Conference security requirements.

Brochure racks will be installed according to your interior design plan. Keeping them attractively filled, and current, is part of whatever system you devise for handling incoming mail.

**Start a
Bookkeeping
System**

Sometime just before the agency opens, or in the early days thereafter, the accountant will instruct you on setting up a bookkeeping system for your agency. To begin with it will be based on the informal records you've kept of monies spent, and the checkbook entries made since acquiring company bank accounts.

All staff members need to know the procedures for recording sales, deposits, handling petty cash, if the accounting system is to work properly. As owner, you may wish to handle the bookkeeping yourself. Even if you choose to hire this service, you should at least become familiar with the system being followed and some of the terminology of travel agency accounting.

**Compile a
Mailing List**

If direct mail is part of your sales promotion plan, you may also have decided to rent the mailing lists you'll use to implement your direct mail campaign.

However, it is considered good practice to begin developing your own house mailing list also, from the beginning of your agency's life. Naturally you'll include the friends, relatives, business contacts, fellow club members that you are counting on to form the nucleus of your beginning clientele.

As an alternative to renting a list, you can make up your own mailing list of local residents at the local library. All you need is their Cole's Directory (in the reference room) and a stack of 3x5 cards.

It's tedious work but not at all difficult. Try to do it just an hour or two at a time or you'll find your card entries becoming sloppy. It's well worth the effort because you can come up with a mailing list that includes just residents within a particular radius, or living on just certain streets, if you wish.

And don't be tempted to make lists of names in lieu of the 3x5 cards. You need the individual cards to cull out duplicates. Eventually you can use them to record individual travel preferences, travel sales, or to divide them into potential and actual customers. Lists of names may be easier at the beginning, but sooner or later they will have to be put on individual cards anyway.

An Open House Party

There's nothing that says you must have an Open House, but it seems to be traditional for new travel agencies. Whether a one-shot affair combining trade people and potential customers, or a series of promotional events, it seems appropriate to mark the occasion in some festive fashion.

Both the Brownell and Gregory books have many ideas in this area. And you probably can think of a few good ideas of your own, or adapt ideas you've seen other retail shops use.

It is standard to invite every sales rep from the airlines, as well as cruise lines, tour companies, etc.—but then not to really expect them all to show up. The invitation just serves to notify them of your impending existence.

I think if I had it to do over, rather than a single open house at the time we submitted our applications, I'd plan a series of weekly promotions instead, directed at local business owners, service organizations and clubs, and residents. In short, I'd concentrate in those early weeks on having as many people and groups as possible participate in some kind of promotion that brought them physically into the agency.

As to letting the travel industry know of my existence, I believe I'd rely on very good looking formal announcements and much telephone contact, and save the open house party until later when I knew my Conference applications would be approved.

Whatever you elect to do, it deserves much thought and planning, not only because it should result in sales prospects, but because the opening period festivities sets a tone and image that can be negative or positive. You need a feeling of momentum in those early weeks both for the goal of travel sales, and for your own morale.

EXHIBIT 10

CHECKLIST: SETTING UP FOR OFFICE OPERATIONS AND TRAVEL SALES

Office Equipment
- Typewriters and Ribbons
- Calculators
- Adding machine and tape
- Letter-size file cabinets
- Legal-size file cabinets
- Locked cabinet; Safe
- Card files for mailing list
- Refrigerator
- Stove or hotplate
- Coffeemaker, teakettle
- Vacuum cleaner or Carpetsweeper
- Desk trays, accessories
- Wastebaskets
- Clocks, calendars
- Cleaning supplies

Travel Sales Supplies
- Airline reservation cards
- Travel order worksheets
- Hotel reservation forms
- Itinerary worksheets and forms
- Vouchers
- Receipts
- Group travel worksheets
- Client interest forms
- Client evaluation forms
- Fam Trip evaluation forms
- Carbonset memos
- 800 Number Directories
- Travel Posters and Displays
- Other:_____

  _____

Office Supplies
- Imprinted stationery and business cards
- Bond and onionskin paper
- Carbon paper
- File folders, dividers, tabs
- Pens, pencils
- Paper clips, tacks
- Rubber bands
- Scissors, rulers
- Tape of various kinds
- Staplers and staples
- KoRecType, fluid and tape
- 3x5, 5x8 cards and dividers
- Supplies for bookkeeping and accounting system

Travel Brochures and Information
- Airlines
- Steamship and Cruise Lines
- Hotels, Motels, Resorts
- Tour Operators
- Railroads, U.S. and Other
- Freighter Travel
- Car Rental and Leasing
- Sightseeing
- Motorcoach
- Transfer Services
- Traveler Insurance
- Traveler's Checks
- Limousine Services
- Special Interest Travel
- Group and Incentive Travel
- Convention Arrangements

EXHIBIT 10, continued

Miscellaneous
   National Tourist Office Information
   Maps, City Guides
   Guidebooks
   Cruise Tips, Deck Plans
   Customs Information and Forms
   Immunization Information and Forms
   Passport, Visa, Tourist Card Information and Forms
   Packing and Clothes Tips

   Language Study Records
   Foreign Phrase Books
   Currency Converters
   Time Converters
   Giveaways: Luggage Tags, Flight Bags, etc.
   Other:_____

NOTES:

1) Travel Industry Reference Materials: These are listed, with addresses for ordering, in Appendix B, thus they are not repeated here. Current price and ordering information should be obtained as part of Phase One.

2) Other Conferences: You should also have necessary forms and information on hand for applying for appointment by IPSA, TPPC, AMTRAK.

3) Ticket stock and airline ticketing forms, information on the mechanized reporting system and Area Bank will be received as a normal part of your appointment procedures for ATC and IATA.

4) Exchange Orders are obtained from individual airlines and can be used for ordering airline tickets until you are officially appointed by ATC and IATA.

5) Depending on your window display plans, you need various supplies to mount or hang displays and to change the display periodically.

6) If you are going to prepare any camera-ready copy as part of your promotion and advertising plans you need additional supplies obtainable at a good art supply store: carbon typewriter ribbons, rub-off letters, burnishing tool, non-photo blue pencils, T-square, steel-edged ruler, razor blades, gum eraser, rubber cement, etc.

Phase Five

Application for Appointment

Phase Five begins when you are ready to file your applications with ATC and IATA. It can be the day after your grand opening, or you can postpone filing them until the agency has functioned for a while.

I can see no advantage in postponing submission of the applications and ideally, it seems to me, they should be ready to go the day you're open for business.

If you've followed earlier suggestions the rough draft answers for both the ATC and IATA applications should be pretty much completed. The work you'll do now is to thoroughly check your answers, and prepare the final assembly of cover letter, applications and enclosures and send them off to ATC and IATA.

Then comes the waiting-it-out period when you'll be inspected by the Conferences and, if all goes well, in about three months you will be formally added to the Agency List.

As said earlier, this can be a trying time. Perhaps you'll be fortunate enough to have so much business the time will fly by without anxiety. More typically, it will be a relatively slow time until your travel sales gradually build.

Therefore, it would be well to have a list of projects in mind to keep you busy, whenever travel sales are a bit slow. Not only is it a good idea for your own morale, but it's probably the one time in your agency's life when you will have some time to spare.

The ATC Application

The ATC application process may seem more complicated than IATA's because of all the enclosures involved. Actually, it's simpler because the questionnaire can be answered in many instances with a simple yes or no. However, if you answer some questions—such as II E—with a yes, be prepared to provide a good mitigating explanation.

1) Check your rough draft of the application and fill in any incomplete or missing answers.

2) Have it typed up in final form, being careful not to separate any of the six pages from its duplicate. Be sure also that the carbon is inserted correctly so you end up with one copy that is all original and one that is all a carbon (this means flipping the pages and carbon when you type 2, 4 and 6).

3) If you haven't already done so, prepare the enclosures:
   Fill in the agency ID plate order form by hand
   Type in information on ATC Sales Agency Agreement (one copy is a card; one is letter-sized)
   Type the Ticket Imprinter Purchase Order
   Type the Ticket Stock Requisition Form (ATC sets the amounts you merely complete the rest)
   Type the three address labels

4) Assemble the various documents acquired over the past weeks from your ATC file:
   Two voided bank checks from ATC Bank account
   Financial statement and bank verification
   The approved bond
   Reference letters attesting to ERP experience
   Photographs, one interior and one exterior

5) Write a cover letter to ATC in which you list, in detail, each item you are transmitting per ATC application checklist

6) Write checks for the ATC application fee and for the imprinter; staple the first to the cover letter, the second to the Ticket Imprinter Purchase Order.

7) Have the application signed and notarized, the Agency Sales Agreement signed and witnessed. Check to see that you have a copy for your files of every item assembled. Some items may need a copy made and for some you may already have a carbon.

8) Assemble the entire ATC application as per Exhibit 11, check it once again for accuracy and completeness, and mail it, packed flat, via certified mail with a return receipt requested, when you mail off the IATA application.

9) In addition to a retained copy of every item forwarded to ATC, your permanent file should now contain:
    The application checklist
    Various instruction sheets
    Sheet entitled "Mechanized Reporting" with Attachment 1 (Attachment 2 you gave to the bank)
    ATC Resolution 80.10
    Text of the Agency Sales Agreement

The IATA Application

IATA requires that you answer a long series of questions on your agency letterhead, rather than on the form itself. Some of the questions require narrative answers. Typing this application in final form is not a job for a mediocre typist. If your skills are limited to filling out travel forms or typing a short postcard or letter now and then, hire someone to do the job.

You do not need to type out each question before each reply. Simply note the number and letter of the question. Be sure that you keep track and that your numbers and letters are correct because it is the only way to identify a particular answer.

Question 12 may pose a problem. We put $100,000 because that seemed to be IATA's minimum.

Question 32 requires only a brief reply, but then asks that you include the entire following page, verbatim, as part of your application. We were so super-careful, we did just that—typed it verbatim. However, I don't know why a photocopy wouldn't do just as well.

1) Check your rough draft of answers to the questionnaire, filling in any that are incomplete or missing. Check to be sure the answers are correctly identified by number and/or letter. And, since you might as well make an intelligent impression, check to be sure there are no errors in spelling, punctuation and grammar in your lengthier responses.

2) Have it typed in final form and proofread for correctness.

3) Assemble the enclosures:
   Statement of Assets and Liabilities (if over 6 months old, it must be updated)
   Photographs
   Promotional material submitted as evidence of sales promotion ability

4) Write a cover letter, listing each item being transmitted

5) Write a check for application, entrance and annual fees as stated in IATA's cover letter.

6) Have all required signatures entered and notarized, and see that you have a copy for your file of everything being sent forward.

7) Assemble the entire package as per Exhibit 11. Check once again for accuracy and completeness. Pack flat and send it off to IATA, certified mail, with return receipt requested.

8) In addition to a retained copy of every item forwarded to IATA, your permanent file should contain:
   IATA's cover letter
   The questionnaire
   General Information to Applicants
   Important Notice—Financial Requirements
   Statement of International Air Passenger Transportation Sales
   Excerpts from Resolution 810a

What Happens Now?

Once you get your slips back from the post office letting you know that IATA and ATC have received the applications safely, you simply settle your mind down for the long wait. Check the mail each day so that a possible letter from either Conference doesn't get buried in the avalanche of brochures you receive. We did receive a nice letter from ATC shortly after sending the application advising us of what to expect, and also asking for some additional information not part of the original instructions. I don't remember that we ever heard a word from IATA until we were finally approved and received their form letter of instructions to newly appointed agencies.

If you are unlucky enough to have any change in status of ownership or persons whose experience is qualifying you for appointment, advise both Conferences immediately. I say unlucky, because such an event would undoubtedly delay your appointment process considerably.

Soon you'll start receiving unannounced inspection visits from airline sales reps. At this writing there were plans to turn these inspections over to an outside company, rather than using airline personnel, and that system may well be in effect by the time your agency is established.

If all is well, in about six weeks you should start to receive unmistakable signs that something is happening—but it all sort of dribbles in. The validator comes from the manufacturer, the ATC Handbook arrives, and the Tariff. A letter or brochure comes across your desk that has a number very much like the agency code number you'll eventually receive. And so it goes.

Eventually, you'll receive it all—agency plate, ticket stock, and formal notification that you are on the Agency List. You still need the individual plates from each ATC and IATA airline before you can actually write tickets. Theoretically, each airline is free to acknowledge you or not, but practically speaking, once appointed by ATC the airlines are all only too happy to have you sell and write tickets for their airline.

Sales Productivity

If you remember, IATA asked for an estimate of international airline sales you expected to make for the first year and beyond. They also provided you with a form for reporting your sales.

We did not submit a sales report in 60 days as IATA suggests. However, one of the inspectors from an international airline did ask to examine our records of airline sales and noted the information in his report. So you must keep accurate up-to-date records of all airline sales, domestic and international, both for possible inspection and for claiming retroactive commissions once appointed.

Following appointment to the list, a letter received from IATA contained this statement:

"You are advised that the IATA Agency Administration Board has agreed that if an Agent attains $100,000 in gross annual sales of international air transportation, this will ensure that such Agent will be retained as an IATA Approved Agent on the Automatic Productivity Review."

ATC's policy on this matter is contained in Par.16 of the Agency Sales Agreement (See Appendix C).

Living in Limbo   During these weeks—as long as three months, actually—you will, of course, be running a travel agency, open to the public, exactly as you will be doing after your appointments arrive. The only difference is that you cannot write airline tickets during this interim period.

If business is slow during these opening months, there are still many, many things to do, and projects to start, to fill the working day.

1) Simply maintaining an office routine is a primary task. Opening up on time each day, picking up mail, stamping and filing brochures, keeping brochure racks in order, bookkeeping and banking chores, etc. are chores that go on day after day no matter how busy you are.

2) You can file your applications for appointment to IPSA and TPPC. As I remember, IPSA did not come through with their appointment until we'd received ATC's imprimatur, but were quite willing to take requests for information and possible steamship reservations in the interim.

3) If at all possible, have at least one person attend a seminar on the Mechanized Sales Report system. Ordinarily you cannot attend airline training seminars until after appointment but exceptions are sometimes made if a sales rep recommends it.

4) Write to ASTA, ARTA and ICTA and find out membership requirements and opportunities you can avail yourself of now and once appointed. Actual membership may have to await appointment or some specified length of time.

5) Continue the sales promotion and advertising campaign begun as part of your opening up process. The samples you sent to IATA should be just the beginning of a long-range continuing program.

6) If you haven't done so yet, spend some time at the library and make up a hand-tailored house mailing list for your agency from Cole's Directory.

7) Compile lists of clubs, organizations, key people in these organizations, for possible sales promotion of group travel.

8) Begin work on some special tour you would like your Agency to offer.

9) Interview, hire and train your cadre of outside sales reps, if you plan to move in this direction.

10) Develop and have typed a policy and procedures manual.

11) Review the travel background of all staff members and make a list of cities or countries not yet visited. Although RRT is not available for a year following appointment, and most reduced fares for cruises and fam trips must await appointment sometimes you can participate in tours during this interim period. Be on the alert as you read the mail for any possible travel opportunities open to your staff now and during the first year.

Brownell's book on travel agency management is loaded with suggestions for worthwhile management activities, so there's really no excuse for sitting around moping on slow days.

A Few Last Details A few final details that need attention once you've received official notification of your appointments:

1) File for the airline commissions you've earned.

2) File necessary forms to qualify for RRT a year from the date of your appointments.

3) Make follow-up calls to ATC and IATA if any part of the equipment or references they indicate should have been received by now have not arrived.

4) Plan an open house just for industry sales reps, or at least advise the airline reps of your appointment and request they deliver the individual airline plates as soon as possible.

5) Follow through on any other appointments (IPSA, TPPC, AMTRAK, etc.), or arrangements with any other principals which may be dependent upon your appointments.

6) Send a press release announcing your appointment as an agency to the trade press.

Final Note A quick reading of this book gives an overview of the mechanics involved in starting a travel agency. Putting the book into practice in a venture of your own, however, means much hard work.

If there's one thought I'd like to leave with you, it is this: don't let inertia, or excessive haste, cause you to short-cut any step of the process. Every phase of the work involved deserves your best efforts and full concentration before going on to the next.

I hope you will find the information herein, and general approach of this Manual to travel agency ownership, to be of help to you.

The best of luck in your new venture!

EXHIBIT 11

CHECKLIST FOR ASSEMBLING ATC AND IATA APPLICATIONS

ATC

Cover letter listing details of each enclosure, with check for application fee stapled to the front
Completed application form, in duplicate
Current financial statement, with bank verification on reverse completed, or a separate bank letter verifying deposits
ATC Sales Agency Agreement: computer card and memo both signed (memo will be returned to you after appointment)
Original of approved bond for minimum of $10,000
Three letters of reference attesting to work experience of person, or persons, listed on application as meeting the experience requirements
Photographs of interior and exterior (staple to 8½ x 11 paper for neater final assembly)
Agency Identification Plate Order Form
Ticket Imprinter Purchase Order Form with check for payment stapled to it
Ticket Stock Requisition Form
Two voided checks on ATC sales remittance account (staple to 8½ x 11 paper)
Typed address labels (restaple as received)

IATA

Cover letter listing details of each enclosure, with check for application, entrance and annual fees stapled to it
Complete replies to all questions, on agency letterhead, in triplicate
A current statement of assets and liabilities (not older than 6 months), on the form provided by IATA
Samples of promotional material (clip and staple neatly to 8½ x 11 paper
8 x 10 photographs of exterior and interior (staple to 8½ x 11 paper)

APPENDIX A

SUGGESTIONS FOR FURTHER READING AND STUDY
(Re-read Exhibit 3)

About Small Business in General

Baumbach, Clifford M., et al. *How to Organize and Operate a Small Business.* Prentice-Hall, 1973.

Breen, George. *Do-it-Yourself Marketing Research.* McGraw-Hill, 1977.

Dible, Donald W. *Up Your Own Organization, A Handbook on How to Start and Finance a New Business.* The Entrepeneur Press, 1974.

Golden, Hal, and Hanson, Kitty. *How to Plan, Produce and Publicize Special Events.* Oceana Pub., 1960.

Greene, Gardiner G. *How to Start and Manage Your Own Business.* McGraw-Hill, 1975.

Latimer, H. C., *Advertising Production Planning and Copy Preparation for Offset Printing.* Five Mile River Pub. Co., 1975.

Roman, Kenneth, and Maas, Jane. *How to Advertise.* St. Martin's Press, 1976.

Saphier, Michael. *Office Planning and Design.* McGraw-Hill, 1968.

——*Planning the New Office.* McGraw-Hill, 1978.

Schwartz, Ted. *The Successful Promoter.* Henry Regnery Co., 1976.

Small Business Reporter. (A series of pamphlets, $1.00 each, obtainable from Bank of America, Dept. 3120, P.O.Box 37000, San Francisco, Ca., 94137)

> *Advertising*
> *Avoiding Pitfalls*
> *Beating the Cash Crisis*
> *Cash Flow/Cash Management*
> *Financing Small Business*
> *Opening Your Own Business: A Personal Appraisal*
> *Steps to Starting a Business*

About the Travel Agency Business in Particular

The following list includes everything I could find *available to non-travel industry people.* Even so, several items mentioned have limited usefulness to the general public either because they are not generally stocked in libraries or because they are very expensive, or both. For this reason I have included the price and publisher's address should you wish to purchase any of them.

Anolik, Alexander. *The Law and the Travel Industry.* Alchemy Books, Box 808, Corte Madera, Ca., 94925. $29.95.
    I haven't read this, but understand it is written by a leading legal expert in the field of travel industry law.

APPENDIX A, continued

Bowers, Norman *How to Open Your Own Travel Agency.* Trav-L Pub., 2698 Waverly St., Palo Alto, Ca., 94306. 1974. $3.95.

    This is the only book I ever came across that was written by a small, retail travel agency owner. It is super-upbeat, and makes turning a new agency into a $1,000,000 annual sales winner, seem like a snap. It is not listed in standard library references, is quite out of date by now, and if you want to read it you'll probably have to try sending to the publisher for it.

Brownell, George, *Travel Agency Management.* Southern University Press, 130 South 19th St., Birmingham, Al., 35233. 1975. $9.75.

    A "must" for new agency owners. To quote from its preface: "Directed primarily to present or prospective managers and owners of retail travel agencies, this book gives detailed suggestions for handling many specific management problems as well as general tips on how to manage a more efficient and more profitable travel agency."

Gregory, Aryear, *The Travel Agent: Dealer in Dreams.* MC Enterprises, 16829 Park Circle Drive, Chagrin Falls, Ohio. $29.95.

    Deals with start-up procedures to some extent, but its great value lies in the comprehensive coverage of travel agency day-to-day operations touching on everything from writing airline tickets to setting up a filing system. The price is high, but I bought it because at the time I was desperate for information and could find no other book just like it.

ICTA, *The Travel Agent and The Law,* Obtainable from ICTA (address given later in this Appendix). $35; $15 for ICTA members.

    Analysis of current court rulings that affect travel agents, with case references provided for lawyers.

Lehman, Armin, *Travel and Tourism, An Introduction to Travel Agency Operations.* Bobbs-Merrill, $12.95.

    I could not get hold of a copy of this book as this Manual went to press. However, Mr. Lehman is one of three leading travel management consultants, writes a column for the trade press, the book is brand new, and undoubtedly worth your reading it. Bobbs-Merrill is a major publisher and the book should be appearing in libraries.

Madden, Dr. Donald L., *Accounting for the Travel Agent* and *Management Accounting for the Travel Agency Executive: ICTA.* $12.95 each. Available from ICTA.

    Used as texts in the ICTA Executive Management course, the second is the more advanced text of the two.

Purvis, F.K., Travel Marketing Consultant Service, 37 Haverford Rd., Hicksville, N.Y., 11801. A series of manuals, obtainable from publisher. $15 each.
    Travel Primer (includes material on new agencies), 1974.
    Official Travel Agency Marketing Handbook (3 parts), 1973-74.

APPENDIX A, continued

Stevens, Laurence. Merton House Pub. Co., 8 South Michigan Avenue, Chicago, Ill., 60603.

Merton House publishes a series of travel agency management books, which fortunately are beginning to appear in libraries. A few are quite new and may not be easily found as yet. You can, however, order any of them from Merton House. They have a brochure describing the series in detail.

Guide to Buying, Selling and Starting a Travel Agency, $9.95.

Invaluable book by an expert in the field who is both travel agent and a travel consultant. Tight, concentrated text, which covers, as title indicates, the pros and cons of buying an existing agency vs starting a new one.

Travel Agent's Guide to Hiring and Supervising, $8.00.

Until the Merton House new series of books were issued (see below) this was the only volume I know of, available to the general public, on the important question of hiring and retaining staff. Vital if you plan to hire an ERP.

Following is a description of a newly-published series by Merton House. I have not personally examined any of them, but include a listing for your information.

Vol. I—*Guide to Travel Agency Accounting*, by M. J. Batham, $12.

Offers a book "which takes the complexity out of travel agency accounting. . .simplified accounting system. . .no expensive forms are required. . ." Written by one who owns a travel agency and also has an accounting degree.

Vol. II—*The Travel Agency Personnel Manual*, by Laurence Stevens, $12.

Includes topics on hiring staff, managing self and staff, interviewing, hiring an agency manager, training new employees. Also has a suggested travel agency policy manual and a self-test "designed to indicate just how good the manager is at managing and what he should do to improve himself."

Vol. III—*Tour Operating--A Guide for Travel Agents*, by John B. Seales, $12.

Since tours and group travel offer the best potential for agency profits, this would seem to be a long-needed addition to the literature available on travel agency management. Publication date is January of this year, so you may not be able to find it at book stores or libraries for a few months. Includes topics on "how to develop and promote a tour. . .create an attractive tour brochure. . .proper pricing. . .how to escort a tour. . .when it is better to sell an existing program. . .documentation. . .where to find prospective group, special interest and other tour business. . ." and more.

Volin, Stan. *How to Become a Sparetime Travel Agent.* Pub. S.Volin, P.O.Box 571 ~~57A~~, Hicksville, N.Y. 11802. 1977. ~~$2.95.~~ 3.25

Not really concerned with management, but its subject may be of special interest to you.

83

APPENDIX A, continued

Small Business Administration Publications

The modest price of these books and pamphlets made them worth a special section of this Appendix. They are available from the Superintendent of Documents, Government Printing Office, Washington, DC, 20402. The free ones can be picked up from your nearest SBA Field Office or SBA, Washington, DC, 20416.

1. *Starting and Managing a Small Business of Your Own*, $2.40
25. *Guides for Profit Planning*, .85
26. *Personnel Management Guides for Small Business*, 1.10
27. *Profitable Community Relations for Small Business*, 1.50
34. *Selecting Advertising Media—A Guide for Small Business*, 2.75

Free Management and Small Marketers Aids

71. Checklist for Going Into Business
111. Interior Display: A Way to Increase Sales
113. Quality and Taste as Sales Appeals
118. Legal Services for Small Retail and Service Firms
121. Measuring the Results of Advertising
152. Using a Traffic Study to Select a Retail Site
153. Business Plan for Small Service Firms
156. Marketing Checklist for Small Retailers
160. Advertising Guidelines for Small Retail Firms
164. Plan Your Advertising Budget
194. Marketing Planning Guidelines
223. Incorporating a Small Business
231. Selecting the Legal Structure for Your Business
233. Planning and Goal Setting for Small Business

There are many, many more—this is simply a sampling of the kind of information available to you free, or at very modest cost, which you can add to your permanent information collection.

APPENDIX A, continued

Education - Courses - Testing Programs

A few years ago ATC came close to mandating that every travel agency have at least one staff member who could pass their proctored examination on geography, general travel information, airline ticketing, tariffs, fares, etc. In the resulting furor and division of opinion within the industry as to its value, fairness and legality, the idea was dropped.

However, anyone going into the business should be aware that it is inevitable travel agencies will be forced to comply with some kind of testing program or Federal licensing regulations, or both. At least it seems to me that some such program is inevitable in view of the wave of consumerism, the increasing number of air travelers, and Ralph Nader's insistence that it is long overdue.

Whether you believe licensing and testing are the answer to upgrading travel agency personnel and operations, it seems sensible to include a continuing education program as a priority in managing your agency. It can be in the form of regular attendance at airline ticketing seminars, fam trips, and/or some of the special industry programs listed below.

ARTA   Has a new program whereby ARTA members will be able to send their untrained new employees, and outside sales reps, to a week-long training class. Fee is $50.

ASTA   Offers a correspondence course (open to all but more reasonable in price for travel agency employees) which covers the basics of being a travel agent—geography, airline ticketing, counseling, steamships, cruises, hotels, etc., etc.

IATA   Another home study course, available for employees of IATA approved agencies. It is my understanding that this is a far more rigorous program than the test originally proposed by ATC, and that it is internationally accepted as a means of certifying travel agency employees. It is not so well known in the States, however, American employees evidently preferring the personal contacts and classroom approach of airline seminars and the TWA Breech Academy. Because of its home study aspect whereby it can be pursued without losing valuable agency time, as well as its reasonable cost, this is worth your investigation. Ask IATA about the IATA/UFTAA Passenger Agents' Professional Training Course.

ICTA   Their Executive Management Travel Education Course is "primarily designed for the travel agency owner-manager, potential manager or seasoned travel industry personnel, although anyone may enroll." In order to earn the designation CTC, however, candidates must acquire five years' experience in the industry, as well as study and pass a five-

APPENDIX A, continued

part academic program. Courses cover travel agency business management, sales management, marketing, domestic and international tourism. The fifth segment requires a research paper or attendance at a seminar and preparation of a written evaluation.

The course work is covered by the group study method, in local meetings of travel agency owners, agents, or other industry members. When a segment has been completed, a group test is given and examination papers are graded by ICTA. The entire Management Course ordinarily would take from 2-3 years. You can pursue your studies on an individual basis if preferred. This may seem like an intimidating program for a new travel agency owner, but I can't think of a better use of your managerial time, than to acquire the knowledge and broad approach to the travel industry that this program offers.

For readers who are not as yet part of the travel industry, but would like to pursue an educational program toward that end, check local community and 4-year colleges for possible courses offered either for credit or as part of their continuing education program.

For a list of colleges and vocational schools that offer training for travel agency employment, see Laurence Stevens' book, *Your Career in Travel and Tourism*.

APPENDIX B

SOURCES
Useful Addresses

This is certainly not a comprehensive list of travel industry addresses—for that you need the *Travel Industry Personnel Directory* (see Reference Books and Subscriptions) or a publication similar to it. I have not included prices either because of their inevitable upward climb. You will have to obtain current prices yourself.

Bonding Companies
- Hess, Egan, Haglitz and L'Hommedieu, 5530 Wisconsin Avenue, Chevy Chase, Md. 20015
- Marsh & McLennan, 1221 Avenue of the Americas, New York, N.Y. 10019
- Victor Schinner, 5028 Wisconsin Avenue, N.W., Washington, D.C. 20016

Books, Guidebooks, Maps, etc.
- Forsyth Travel Library, Box 2975, Shawnee Mission, KS 62201
    Travel reference books (exclusive agent in U.S. for Cook's International Timetable), travel books, maps, travel management books, globes—single source for a wide variety of printed information, send for a catalog. Has plans to also offer maps and worksheets for itineraries, "instant" art for use in producing travel ads and brochures, etc.

Conferences
- Air Transport Converence (ATC), 1709 New York Ave., NW, Washington, D.C. 20006
- AMTRAK, National Railroad Passenger Corp., 955 L'Enfant Plaza North, S.W., Washington, D.C. 20024
- International Air Transport Association (IATA), P.O. Box 550, 1000 Sherbrooke St.,West, Montreal P.Q. Canada H3A2R4
- International Passenger Ship Association (IPSA), 17 Battery Place, N.Y. 10004
- Trans-Pacific Passenger Ship Converence (TPPC), 311 California St., CA, 94104

Consultants
- Mort Kaufman Associates, Box 445, 1000 Palms, CA 92276
- Armin D. Lehman, 309 Santa Monica Blvd., Suite 304, Santa Monica, CA 90401
- LaurenceStevens, 8 S. Michigan Ave., Chicago, IL60603
    Ask the first two also about the training manuals they offer for sale or for rent.

APPENDIX B, continued

Display Equipment and Supplies
Gerwin Corp., Michigan City, IN
Dell Industries, 1 Fairfield Rd., N. Caldwell, N.J. 07006
Wing-Master Co., Inc., 1659 Stephen St., Ridgewood, N.Y. 11227
TA Marketplace, 5616 E. 2nd St., Long Beach, CA 90803 (ask for free pamphlet, *10 Ways to Display Brochures*)

Giveaways and Premiums
Traveler's Checklist, Cornwall Bridge Rd., Sharon, CT 06069
Forsyth Travel Library (listed under Books) also carries guidebooks which can be purchased at a trade discount and used as bon voyage gifts, etc.

Insurance (Errors and Omissions)
C. B. Beardsley, 1100 Franklin Ave., Garden City, N.Y. 11530
S. A. VanDyk, 9052 S. Ashland, Chicago, IL 60620

Office Systems and Supplies
Pengad Co., 57 Oak St., Bayonne, N.J. 07002
Robinson-Ingledue Travel Pub., 5850 Hollywood Blvd., Hollywood, CA 90028
Willow Press, 160 Oak Drive, Syosset, N.Y. 11791
(ARTA and ASTA also have office systems and forms for travel agencies—see under Travel Industry Associations)

Promotion
Sun Travel Services, 2401 Cleveland Rd., West Huron, OH 44839
Has a plan whereby they will provide you with a ready-written travel column to be used exclusively in your area with your agency name and logo

Reference Books and Subscriptions (a few are free upon appointment)
ABC Travel Guides, Old Hill, London Rd, Sunstabel LU63EB, England
ABC's of Travel, from Travel Weekly, 1 Park Avenue, N. Y. 10016
ATC Travel Agent's Handbook
American Express Datamex, P.O. Box 65, Wall St. Station, N.Y. 10005
American Sightseeing International, 1270 Avenue of the Americas, N.Y. 10020
Consolidated Air Tour Manual, 3800 N.E. First Ave., FL 33137
Cook's Continental Timetable (order from Forsyth)
Ford's Travel Guides (Freighter and Cruise Guides), P.O. Box 505, Woodland Hills, CA 91365

APPENDIX B, continued

Gray Line Official Sightseeing Tariff, Gray Line Sightseeing Co., 7 West 51st St., N.Y. 10019
Hotel/Motel Red Book, American Hotel and Motel Assn., 888 Seventh Ave., New York, N.Y. 10019
Hotel and Travel Index, P.O. Box 596, Neptune, N.J. 07753
IATA Ticketing Handbook (from IATA)
International Shipline Guide, 2720 Beverly Blvd., Los Angeles, CA 90057
International Tariff (from IATA)
Jax Fax Charter Guide, 400 Madison Avenue, New York, N.Y.
Manual for Travel Agents on Sale of Steamship Travel (from IPSA)
Michelin Guides and Maps, P.O. Box 188, Roslyn Heights, N.Y. 11577
Mobil Guides, Box 265 Old Chelsea Station, New York, N.Y. 10011
OAG Guides (order from Reuben Donnelley Corp., 2000 Clearwater Dr., Oak Brook, Ill. 60521)
　OAG-North American Edition
　OAG-Worldwide Edition
　OAG World Cruise and Steamship Guide
　OAG Travel Planner and Hotel/Motel Guide
Official Guide of the U.S. Railways, National Railway Co., 424 W. 33d St., New York, N.Y. 10001
Official Hotel & Resort Guide, P.O. Box 2132, Radnor, PA 19089
Official Meeting Facilities Guide, 1 Park Ave., New York, N.Y. 10016
Official Steamship Guide, Transportation Guides, Inc. 299 Madison Ave., New York, NY 10017
Pan Am World Guide and Guide to U.S., Pan Am Publications

Russell's Motorcoach Guide, 817 Second Ave., Cedar Rapids, IA
Squires Tariff, AT Publishers 1825 K St., Washington, D.C. 20005
Star Service, P.O. Box 17205, W. Hartford, CT 06117 (hotels)
Travel Industry Personnel Directory, Travel Agent Magazine, 2 W.46th St., New York, N.Y. 10036
WATA Master Key, World Assn. for Travel Agencies, P.O. Box B852, 1211 Geneva 1, Switzerland
World Travel Directory, P.O. Box 2134, Radnor, PA 19089

Travel Services
Customs Hints for Returning U.S. Citizens, Superintendent of Documents, Washington, D.C.

APPENDIX B, continued

Language Study Tapes and Records-Educational Services, 1730 Eye St., N.W., Washington, D.C. 20006

Tele-Trip (travel insurance) Mutual of Omaha, 313 Dodge St., Omaha, NE

Visa Service-Travel Agenda, 119 W. 57th St., New York, N.Y. 10019

Travel Industry Associations

American Association of Travel Agents, 711 Fifth Ave., N.Y. 10022

Association of Retail Travel Agents, 9 Maple St., Croton-on-Hudson, N.Y., 10520

Institute of Certified Travel Agents (ICTA), 148 Linden St., Wellesley, MA 02181

Trade Publications

The Travel Agent Magazine, 2 West 46th St. New York, N.Y. 10035

TravelAge East, 888 Seventh Ave., N.Y. 10019

TravelAge MidAmerica, 2416 Prudential Plaza, Chicago, IL 60601

TravelAge West, 582 Market St., San Francisco, CA 94104

Travel Scene, Agent's Edition 888 Seventh Ave., New York, NY 10019

Travel Trade, 605 Fifth Ave., N.Y. 10017

Travel Weekly, 1 Park Ave., New York, N.Y. 10016

Toll Free Directories

Traveler's Toll Free Directory, Landmark Publishing, Box 3287N, Burlington, VT 05401

Travel 800, Cabell Travel Publications, 11411 Cumpston St., N. Hollywood, CA 91601

APPENDIX C
(p.91-119)

AIRLINE CONFERENCE APPLICATION INFORMATION

Following is a list of the items you'll receive from ATC and IATA. Items marked with an asterisk, have been reproduced herein, for your information, but not necessarily in the order listed:

ATC—
    Application for Accreditation as Sales Agent for ATC Member Airlines (Instructions)
    Applicant Check List
  *Explanation of ATC Personnel Experience Requirements
    Balance Sheet Form
    Agency Identification Plate Order Form
    ATC Bond Form
    Mechanized Reporting, with two Attachments(check facsimile and Authorization to Honor Checks Drawn by ATC)
  *Excerpts from the ATC Agency Resolution 80.10
    Resolution 80.4, Establishment of Office of Travel Agent Commissioner
  *Applications for Accreditation—Most Frequent Problems; Common Correction Actions; General Principles
  *The Application Form
    Ticket Imprinter Purchase Order
    Ticket Requisition
    Shipping Labels
    Instructions to Applicant (Sales Agency Agreement)
    Memorandum of Sales Agency Agreement computer card, and Memorandum of Sales Agency Agreement (Agent's Copy)
  *Text of the Sales Agency Agreement
    (pp. 1 thru 12 reproduced here)
  *Supplement 1, Resolution 80.15, Standard Travel Agent Finance Statement

IATA—
    General Information to Applicants
    Cover letter of instructions and fees
    Instructions and Questionnaire for Agency Application for the sale of International Air Passenger Transportation (USA)
    Important Notice—Financial Requirements
    Statement of Assets and Liabilities Form
    Statement of International Air Passenger Transportation Sales Form
    Extract from IATA Sales Agency Rules—Approval and Qualification of Agents (Res. 810a, Sec.D,par. 3 and 4)

Above lists represent application kits received as of January, 1979, as does the various excerpts reproduced as part of Appendix C. Check the kits you receive carefully against Appendix C, as well as the text of this Manual. You must adjust your activities to meet whatever changes in requirements occur.

The last item listed under ATC (Standard Travel Agent Finance Statement) is interesting. I had not planned to include it at all in this Manual, and do not mention it at all in the text. The reason is that it was included in the January 1979 kit marked "for information only"—however, just before the Manual went to press it suddenly became a hot issue. Agents are being required by the ATC to sign this document, which gives the airlines first call on agency assets in the case of default. ARTA is strongly opposed to this, and some agencies have refused to sign the document thereby risking cancellation of their airline appointments.

The final outcome was not clear at this writing, but it is a matter which you must be concerned with if it is a definite part of appointment procedures at the time your agency venture is begun.

Following is an index of the reproduced items:

93 - Applications for Accreditation (problems, correction actions, general principles)
94 - Explanation of ATC Personnel Experience Requirements
95-100 - Excerpts from ATC Agency Resolution 80.10 (cross-references are indicated to the application form itself)
101-105 - The application form
106-117 - Text of Sales Agency Agreement (excluding Schedules A,B,C)
118-119 - Schedule D, Standard Travel Agent Finance Statement

APPLICATIONS FOR ACCREDITATION

MOST FREQUENT PROBLEMS

1. Application reveals personnel with significant ties to a previously defaulted agency, leading to ATC disapproval.
2. Manager-designate does not have the two years full-time promotional experience required by the Agency Resolution for new applicants.
3. New applicant fails to obtain ATC approval for a change in the ownership of a previously owned agency, which leads to exploitation and default of the agency in the hands of the unauthorized new owner.
4. Owner has been found to have been devious and untruthful and to have failed to disclose pertinent information concerning his qualifications, leading to ATC disapproval.
5. Failure of existing agent to meet the "full-time" promotional experience requirement.
6. New applicant owned or controlled by a single entity or person with which the agency will do 20 per cent or more of its gross annual air transportation business.

COMMON CORRECTION ACTIONS

1. Confine the functions and powers of person(s) formerly with a defaulted agency to an unobjectionable role with the new applicant as a condition to approval.
2. Replacement of manager-designate, together with the filing of a new application.

GENERAL PRINCIPLES

1. The "full-time" promotional experience standard is not satisfied by sales exposure gained as an incident to extensive airline reservation and ticketing experience. Creative selling performed on a "full-time" basis must be demonstrated to have been the manager's primary responsibility for at least the qualifying two-year period.
2. Strict adherence to ATC change of ownership requirements for advance notice and approval are essential to assure the fitness of new owners and to serve the carriers and the public and to prevent entry of irresponsible operators into the industry.
3. Independent corroboration of an applicant's sales experience is far preferable to self-serving documents or testimony.
4. "Full-time" is interpreted in its generally accepted sense of seven or eight hours per day of worktime in a five day workweek.

10/1/78

EXPLANATION OF ATC PERSONNEL EXPERIENCE REQUIREMENTS

All applicants for ATC approval must have at least one full-time employee staffing the agency location, who meets the experience requirements which are set forth in Section IV.B.10 of the Agency Resolution. A copy of this portion of the Resolution is included in the Excerpts attached hereto, and an explanation of these requirements is spelled out in Part IV of the ATC questionnaire.

Your answer to PART IV.A.2, which covers <u>promotional</u> selling experience, is supposed to explain <u>clearly</u> that the person listed was engaged on a <u>full-time</u> basis in promotional sales work for at least two years. Showing only the person's previous title is not sufficient - you must describe his or her specific job duties. The use of cryptic phrases such as "ticket sales", "promotion", "reservations", "planning itineraries", "ATC Sales Reports", etc. is not sufficient. It must be clearly shown that the person was not merely a ticket writer, order taker, or simply servicing established accounts. The information provided must demonstrate that the person's primary duties, for at least two years' on a full-time basis, involved creative sales work - e.g. <u>generating new sales, promoting destinations, or otherwise inducing people to travel</u>.

With regard to airline ticketing experience, the person listed must have had at least one year's full-time ticketing experience while employed by an ATC/IATA airline or travel agency, within the past three years. The name and address of employer, dates of employment (including month and year), and a description of the specific duties involved - not just a title, should be stated. Since the ticketing experience must have been acquired <u>within the past three years</u>, there is no need to list ticketing experience prior to that period.

3/77
REV: 10/78
12/78

EXERPTS FROM THE AIR TRAFFIC
CONFERENCE AGENCY RESOLUTION 80.10

Cross References
to Applicant
Questionnaire

SECTION 1 DEFINITIONS

AA. The term "Commissioner" means the Travel Agent Commissioner established pursuant to Resolution 80.4.

PART II
D. The term "Agent" means any person included on the Agency List for the purpose of selling air passenger transportation (other than an officer or employee of such Member, or a General Agent appointed by such Member in accordance with the terms of this Resolution, or another common carrier which is legally permitted to engage in passenger and/or freight transportation, but not excluding any person who is an indirect air carrier whose operations are governed by the Special Regulations of the Civil Aeronautics Board (Code of Federal Regulations, title 14, Chapter II, subchapter D). For the purpose of Section VII.A., B and I of this Resolution, "Agent" shall include all parent and subsidiary authorized agency locations and all authorized agency locations under common control.

PART I.D
I. The term "authorized agency location" means a place of business operated by an Agent, which place of business is included on the ATC Agency List. Such location will be the home office if it owns and operates "additional authorized agency locations" as branches of that entity. The term "additional authorized agency location" means a "branch office" location included on the ATC Agency List which is wholly owned and operated as an integral part of the home office and which performs substantially the same promotion and sales functions as the home office, which shall include, but not be limited to the following:
 (1) quoting fares, rates and/or schedules,
 (2) making reservations,
 (3) accepting payment for travel,
 (4) arranging for delivery of tickets or other transportation documents,
 (5) assisting clients with other travel arrangements,
 (6) arranging for the issuance of ticket or other travel documents,
 (7) issuing tickets or other travel documents.
The corporate structure or ownership of the home office and branch(es) must be absolute and all inclusive as a single entity and the home office shall have full legal and financial responsibility for the administration, staff, liability, maintenance and operational expense of the branch office location.
J. The term "bank travel department" means a special department operated by a bank exclusively for the sale of passenger transportation and general travel services, such as tour itineraries, sightseeing arrangements, and hotel reservations, and which is open to the public for such purposes.

P. The term "Member" means any Member of the Conference who is bound by this Resolution pursuant to the By-laws of the Conference.
Q. The term "person" includes an individual, corporation, partnership, association, company, or firm.
R. The term "Sales Agency Agreement" means the Air Traffic Conference Sales Agency Agreement, as shown in Resolution 80.15.
S. The term "transportation bureau" means a place of business, located in a hotel or club, which is operated on a year-around basis (unless it is operated by an Agent who operates at least ten authorized agency locations

PART III
at other addresses on a year-around basis) exclusively for the promotion and sale of passenger transportation and general travel services, such as tour itineraries, sightseeing arrangements, and hotel reservations, and which is open to the public for such purposes; the ownership and management of which are completely independent of the ownership and management of such hotel or club; in the income of which such hotel or club has no financial interest (other than the collection of rent for the space occupied); and none of the operators or employees of which perform any services of the type commonly referred to as "porter services".

DEFINITIONS (continued)

PART III

T. The term "travel bureau" means a place of business which is engaged solely in the promotion and sale of passenger transportation and general travel services, such as tour itineraries, sightseeing arrangements, and hotel reservations and which is open to the public for such purposes; a substantial portion of the income of which is derived from such business; and which is advertised and otherwise represented as an office for the sale of passenger transportation and services related thereto. The words "engaged solely in" apply only with respect to the office, department, or space which the applicant purports to be the travel bureau. An office located in a hotel or club shall not constitute a "place of business" within the meaning of this paragraph. An office located in a private residence which is also used for residential purposes shall not constitute a "place of business" within the meaning of this paragraph, unless such office is used exclusively for business purposes and is open to the public for such purposes; but no such office shall constitute a "place of business" within the meaning of this paragraph if it is operated and maintained by a person who operated a transportation bureau or a travel bureau at another address, or who is employed by any transportation company, or who, as an employee or otherwise, performs any services of the type commonly referred to as "porter services" at any hotel or club.

V. The term "designated area bank" means a bank, and/or a processing contractor designated to receive and process sales reports and remittances from authorized agency locations in a designated geographic area, in accordance with the provisions of Paragraph 5 of the Sales Agency Agreement: Provided, That no bank and/or processing contractor which owns, controls, is controlled by, or is under common control with an authorized agency location shall be designated or continue to be designated, as an area bank.

Y. The term "In-Plant location" means an additional authorized agency location which is on the premises of a customer. An In-Plant location need not be open to the public.

Z. The term "control" means the power or authority to manage, direct, superintend, restrict, regulate, govern, administer, or oversee; and the term embraces every form of control, actual or legal; direct or indirect; negative or affirmative; individual, joint, several, or family; without regard to the type or number of intervening or supervening persons involved. Two persons are under "common control" when a third person(s) controls both.

SECTION IV. THE SELECTION AND RETENTION OF AGENTS IN THE U. S.

A. The Executive Secretary shall maintain, for the information of the Members, an Air Traffic Conference Agency List which shall be kept current, shall show for each authorized agency location a code number assigned by the Executive Secretary, and shall be published at such intervals and in such manner as the Agency Committee may from time to time prescribe. The names of Agents and authorized agency locations shall be placed on, and removed from, the Agency List only as provided in this Section. No Member shall retain any person as its Agent or any place of business as an authorized agency location, unless such person and such location appear on the Agency List then in effect. The Agency List in effect on the effective date of this Section shall continue in effect except as names and/or locations are added, deleted or changed in accordance with this Section. In the event the Executive Secretary shall furnish information from the Agency List to non-participants in the Agent's Standard Ticket and Area Settlement Plan for solicitation purposes, the agent shall be provided the opportunity to have his name and address deleted from the information so provided.

B. Any person who desires to be named as an Agent on the Agency List, or to have any place of business added to the Agency List as an authorized agency location, shall make written application to the Executive Secretary. The application shall be on a standard form, as prescribed from time to time by the Agency Committee, shall be under oath, and shall include, or be accompanied by, the following:
   1. Name in which, and address at which, the business is being conducted;
   2. Form of business entity (proprietorship, partnership, corporation);
   3. Name of each person having a financial or ownership interest in the applicant;
   4. The applicant's current financial statement, with verification of bank balances;
   5. A bond, in the standard ATC form, in the amount of $10,000, or an undertaking by a surety to issue such bond upon receipt of notice that the applicant has been found eligible for inclusion on the Agency List, such bond to be procured and maintained without expense to the Air Traffic Conference of America and/or its Members;

PART II.E
   6. If any person holding a financial or ownership interest in the applicant, or employed by it in any capacity, has or had a connection or affiliation with, or a financial interest in, or was employed by, any Agent previously cancelled from the Agency List, a full statement covering such prior and present connections;

PART III
   7. A concise description of the premises, in sufficient detail to show that the applicant is a travel bureau, transportation bureau, or a bank travel department, as those terms are defined herein, and that the premises are not in a location disqualified under Section IV.L. of this Resolution; and interior and exterior photographs of the premises; and satisfactory evidence that the applicant has made arrangements for and agreed to meet the industry's minimum safeguards to protect airline ticket stock, identification plates and other standard ticket

PART V forms as set forth in Schedule B of the Sales Agency Agreement.

   8. Data showing the appliicant is not owned or controlled by a single entity or person with which the applicant does or will do 20% or more of his gross transportation yearly business as prohibited by Section IV.L of this Resolution.
   9. An application fee as specified in Resolution 80.35;
   10. Evidence that

PART IV
   a. The owner, a partner, an officer or the manager of the applicant has had two years full-time experience in creating, generating and promoting passenger transportation sales and services related thereto (as distinguished from airline ticketing and reservation experience provided for in subsection B.10.c hereunder)
   b. The foregoing person devotes all, or substantially all, of his time, to the management and administration of the agency location and to the promotion and sale of passenger transportation, for the location which the application is intended, provided that a person spending at least 35 hours per week performing such duties shall not be deemed to have met the "substantially all of his time" requirement; and
   c. The foregoing person or another full-time employee of the applicant staffing the location for which the application is intended has had, within the past three years, one year's full-time experience in airline passenger ticketing in the employment of either an ATC or IATA member airline or of a travel agency included on the ATC or IATA Agency Lists. Any tenure of service with one employer for less than six months will not be considered in meeting this requirement.
   11. Letters from former employers or business associates, certifying to the previous work experience in the sale and/or ticketing of passenger transportation and services related thereto, of the individual(s) being relied upon to meet the experience requirements set forth in Section IV.B.10, above;

PART VI
   12. A waiver of any and all rights of action based on libel, slander, or defamation of character by reason of such publication of asserted grounds or reasons for disapproval of such application as is reasonbly related to the performance of appropriate functions specified in applicable Conference Resolutions, as well as an undertaking to be bound by the decision of an arbitral tribunal, as provided in this Resolution.
   13. A "Standard Travel Agent Finance Statement" as set forth in Schedule D, Supplement I of the Sales Agency Agreement, Resolution 80.15, executed by the applicant.

97

SELECTION AND RETENTION (continued)

C. Promptly upon receipt of a fully executed application, the Executive Secretary shall notify all Members of the receipt thereof and shall institute an investigation to verify the statements in that application and to determine whether there is any reason to believe that the applicant does not meet the requirements of this Resolution for inclusion on the Agency List. Upon completion of such investigation, but in no event sooner than 30 days, nor more than 90 days, after receipt of the application, the Executive Secretary shall (unless Section IV.D is applicable), as agent for and on behalf of all Members, enter into a Sales Agency Agreement with such person, and shall place the name of such person on the Agency List and notify all Members of the date on which the execution of such Agreement is completed.

D. 1. The Executive Secretary shall disapprove any applicant where investigation reveals, or he otherwise has reason to believe, that there is a material misrepresentation or inaccuracies in the application or any attachments thereto, or, that the applicant fails to meet the requirements of this Resolution.

PART II. E

2. The Executive Secretary shall disapprove any applicant where he has reason to believe that any person holding a financial or ownership interest in the applicant, or employed by it in any capacity; (a) has or had a connection or affiliation with, or financial interest in, or was employed by, any Agent previously cancelled from the Agency List, or, (b) has been adjudged bankrupt, or is the subject of pending bankruptcy proceedings, or, (c) has been convicted of a felony, or has been convicted of a misdemeanor related to financial activities or a breach of fiduciary duty involving the use of the funds of others, or (d) has been denied application for a travel agent license by any governmental authority, or has had a travel agent license suspended, revoked or cancelled by any governmental authority, or (e) is presently under suspension or pending action of any kind by the Commissioner, (f) unless, based upon investigation, experience of the Members with such person(s), where applicable, and all information and facts available, determines that the applicant can be relied on to adhere to the terms of the Sales Agency Agreement.

PART III

3. The Executive Secretary shall disapprove any application where investigation reveals, or he otherwise has reason to believe, that the place of business covered by the application is not actually in operation as a travel bureau, transportation bureau, or bank travel department, or that the premises are in a location disqualified under Section IV.L of this Resolution, or that the applicant is disqualified under the second or last sentences of Section IV.L: Provided, That the Executive Secretary may in exceptional cases approve not more than one place of business in any city or town not a part of a larger metropolitan area where no authorized agency location exists, as an authorized agency location, even though such place of business is not a bank travel department, transportation bureau, or travel bureau, or is in a location disqualified under Section IV.L. as long as such place of business, in the opinion of the Executive Secretary, does not conflict with the activities of any previously authorized agency location.

PART VI

4. The Executive Secretary shall inform any applicant which is disapproved hereunder the reasons therefor, and shall set forth the basis on which determination was made that such applicant, or the place of business covered by the application, fails to meet the requirements of this Resolution, or that such applicant cannot be relied on to adhere to the terms of the Sales Agency Agreement.

5. Any person who shall deem himself aggrieved by reasons of the disapproval of his application by the Executive Secretary shall have the right to refer such disapproval to the Commissioner for his review in accordance with Resolution 80.4, subject to the following conditions:

(a) Within 30 days after receipt by applicant of notice from the Executive Secretary that his application has been disapproved, the applicant shall notify the Executive Secretary by certified or registered mail of his request to have such disapproval reviewed by the Commissioner. A copy of such request shall be directed to the Commissioner by the applicant by certified or registered mail.

(b) Upon receipt of such written request, the Commissioner shall schedule a review proceeding in accordance with the provisions of Resolution 80.4.

SELECTION AND RETENTION (continued)

6. Any person who shall deem himself aggrieved by reasons of the Commissioner's disapproval of his application shall have the right of appeal to an independent arbitral tribunal subject to the following terms and conditions:
    (a) *Selection of Arbiters:*
        Within 30 days after receipt by applicant of notice from the Commissioner that his application has been disapproved, the applicant shall notify the Executive Secretary by certified or registered mail of his desire to appeal such disapproval to an arbitral tribunal and shall at the same time, name one arbiter acceptable to the applicant. Such notice shall enclose the amount of $100.00 as a deposit toward the applicant's share of the expenses of arbitration. Within 10 days after receipt of such notice from applicant, the Executive Secretary shall name an arbiter acceptable to the Executive Secretary, notifying applicant, by certified or registered mail of the person so selected. Within 20 days after mailing of such notice by the Executive Secretary, the two arbiters so selected shall designate a third, who shall serve as chairman of the tribunal. If such third arbiter shall not have been designated within 90 days after date of mailing by the Executive Secretary of notice that the application has been rejected, such third arbiter shall be designated by the American Arbitration Association.
    (b) *Conduct of Appeal:*
        The tribunal so selected shall set the matter down for hearing not later than thirty days after selection of the chairman and shall notify the Executive Secretary and the applicant of the time and place of such hearing by certified or registered mail; Provided, That at the request of the applicant the date of hearing may be postponed until after the next review by the Commissioner so as to permit him to reconsider his prior action. In the conduct of proceedings before the tribunal, the rules and procedures of the American Arbitration Association, insofar as they are applicable and are not in conflict with this Resolution, shall govern. The decision of a majority of the arbiters shall be final and binding upon both the applicant and the Conference. The expenses of arbitration, including any fees payable to the arbiters, shall be shared equally by the applicant and the Conference.
    (c) *Scope of Appeal:*
        Review by the arbitral tribunal shall be appellate and not de novo. The tribunal shall affirm the decision of the Commissioner unless it finds and concludes that the Commissioner's decision is deficient in one or more of the following respects:
        (i) it is not supported by substantial evidence;
        (ii) new evidence is available to the tribunal which for good cause was not presented to the Commissioner;
        (iii) it contains errors of applicable law;
        (iv) it is arbitrary or capricious; or
        (v) it is not in accordance with the terms of this Resolution or Resolution 80.4.
        In the event the arbitral tribunal does not affirm the decision of the Commissioner, the tribunal shall either direct action upon the applicant in accordance with the tribunal's findings, or remand the matter to the Commissioner for action consistent with the arbitral tribunal's decision.

E. After receipt of notice from the Executive Secretary that execution of a Sales Agency Agreement with a person has been completed, any Member may deliver to such person airline identification plates for use at authorized agency locations: *Provided, that* any Member may withdraw its airline identification plate(s) from any authorized agency location at any time.

F. If the application covers an additional authorized agency location to be operated by an Agent already on the Agency List, the procedures set forth in Sections IV.C and IV.D, shall be followed, with the following exceptions:
    1. The information required by Sections IV.B.6 and IV.B.10 shall be submitted with respect to personnel manning the additional agency locations; and
    2. The Executive Secretary will not execute a separate Sales Agency Agreement, but will promptly advise the applicant and all Members when the additional authorized agency location is added to the Agency List.

SELECTION AND RETENTION (continued)

H. The bond required to accompany the application pursuant to Section IV.B. shall be maintained in the minimum amount of $10,000 so long as the Agent remains on the Agency List, and the amount of the bond shall be increased whenever necessary so as to cover the average of the three highest months (of the last 12) gross sales of air transportation for the account of ATC Members, or, if the Agent has been on the Agency List less than 12 months, the average of the three highest months sales since the Agent was placed on the List. On and after January 1, 1963, all Agents and agency locations on the Agency List shall be required to procure and maintain such bond: *Provided,* That (1) no Agent shall be required to maintain a bond in excess of $50,000; (2) Agents qualifying under the net worth requirement of Paragraph 5 of the Sales Agency Agreement, Resolution No. 80.15 shall be required to maintain only the minimum $10,000 bond; and (3) after the Agent has been on the Agency List for one year, adjustment to provide the required coverage in excess of the $10,000 minimum shall be made at least once a year, and at any other time when the amount of the Agent's bond fails by $2,000 or more to provide the required coverage. Nothing herein shall be deemed to preclude an Agent from reducing the amount of coverage whenever considerations of his sales experience for the most recent twelve consecutive months shows him to be carrying a bond in excess of that herein required.

PART III

L. No place of business shall be included on the Agency List if it is located in an airline terminal, or at an airport, unless the location shall have been placed on the Agency List prior to July 19, 1977, (as used herein, the term airport means the airport and supporting facilities, including all parking areas, under the direct jurisdiction of the airport authorities) or in a hotel unless the place of business has a street-front location with access from the street by means of a door opening directly from the street and not requiring passage through any portion of the hotel: Provided, That the foregoing limitation with respect to locations in a hotel shall not apply to agency locations in Hawaii. No place of business shall be included on the Agency List where it appears that the Agent is owned or controlled by a single entity or person with which the Agent does or will do 20 per cent or more of his gross air transportation yearly business as Agent. In determining whether the Agent does or will do 20 per cent or more of his gross air transportation yearly business with such single entity or person, all business shall be considered which is done by the Agent with such entity or person or with the officers, directors, stockholders, members or employees of such entity or person: *Provided, However,* That any Agent (or his successor in ownership) whose business was conducted in compliance with the Agency Resolution of the Conference in force immediately prior to the effective date of this Paragraph shall be exempt from meeting any qualification set forth in this Paragraph to the extent and degree that such Agent shows that he did not meet such qualification prior to the effective date of this Paragraph; and, *Further Provided,* That any place of business which is not within 20 miles of any other authorized agency location shall not be rejected because of location in a hotel. No applicant shall be included on the Agency List where the applicant has not made arrangements for and agreed to meet the industry's minimum safeguards to protect airline ticket stock, identification plates and other standard ticket forms as set forth in Schedule B of the Standard Agents Ticket and Area Settlement Plan. No place of business shall be included or retained on the Agency List where it appears that the Agent or applicant does or will do 20 per cent or more of its gross air transportation yearly business, in the aggregate, as Agent with itself and/or any other person(s) which controls, is controlled by or is under common control with, the Agent. In determining whether the Agent or applicant is or will be disqualified under the aforementioned limitation, all business shall be considered which is or will be done by the Agent or applicant with itself and/or such other person(s) which controls, is controlled by, or is under common control with, the Agent, or with the officers, directors, stockholders, members or employees of the Agent and/or such other persons.

PART V

PART II. D

N. During the pendency of an application for approval of an additional authorized agency location, an Agent may deliver at the location covered by said application tickets or exchange orders written up and validated at an approved location of the Agent, provided that the Agent has the written consent of the Member whose airline identification plate is used on such tickets, which consent shall not be given until after receipt by the Member of notice from the Executive Secretary that said application has been duly filed with him.

PART I. D

O. No location shall be included on the Agency List as an additional authorized agency location unless the corporate structure or ownership of the home office and the branch is absolute and all-inclusive as a single entity, and the home office has full legal and financial responsibility for the administration, staff, liability, maintenance and operational expense of the branch office location.

100

(4th Rev. 9/74 - 178)

APPLICATION FOR ACCREDITATION AS AN ATC SALES AGENT
(4th Rev. 9/74 - 178)
AIR TRAFFIC CONFERENCE OF AMERICA
1709 New York Ave., N.W. • Washington, D.C. 20006

FOR ATC USE ONLY

APPLICANT QUESTIONNAIRE

The information requested below is required by the Air Traffic Conference in order to determine your eligibility for inclusion on the ATC Agency List. Answer in full Parts I through VI and submit the completed questionnaire in duplicate (original and one copy) along with all required enclosures outlined on the accompanying Instruction Sheet—i.e., application fee, financial statement, photographs, etc. APPLICATIONS MUST BE COMPLETE IN ALL RESPECTS BEFORE PROCESSING CAN BEGIN. NO CONSIDERATION WILL BE GIVEN TO AN INCOMPLETE APPLICATION. PLEASE TYPE OR PRINT CLEARLY. BE SURE TO RETAIN AN EXTRA COPY OF THIS QUESTIONNAIRE FOR YOUR PERMANENT RECORD.

PART I. DESIGNATION OF AGENCY LOCATION

A. Give the full legal name, including trade name(s) if any, the complete address and telephone number of the office for which this application is intended:

B. Has the above location been approved by the International Air Transport Association (IATA)? .... ☐ YES ☐ NO

If so, give month & year of approval _____, and the IATA assigned Agency Code Number _____

C. If not, do you presently have an application for approval of the above location pending with IATA?... ☐ YES ☐ NO

D. Is the above location a BRANCH OFFICE of, i.e., wholly owned by, a presently approved ATC agency? . ☐ YES ☐ NO

If so, give full name, address and telephone no. of your HOME OFFICE, its ATC Agency Code Number and date of ATC Approval.

_____ Code No. _____
_____ Tel. No. _____
_____ Approval Date _____

Note: An additional (branch) office of an ATC approved agency must list in I.A. above, the same primary or corporate name as its headquarters office, but may also include a trade name if so desired.

PART II. OWNERSHIP STATUS OF AGENCY

A. Check type of ownership entity:
☐ Proprietorship; ☐ Partnership; ☐ Corporation (state when and where incorporated): _____

B. List name(s), residence address(es) and home telephone number(s) of the owner, or each partner, or, if corporation, each stockholder as well as non-stockholding officers or directors, if any. Include titles for each, i.e., owner, partner, president, etc., and indicate the percentage of time each is expected to devote to the day-to-day operation of the agency and the percent of stock held, if a corporation. If more space is needed, use PART VII of this form.

Name & Title	Residence Address & Telephone Number	% of Time to Agency	% of Stock Held

101

C. Do any of the above named persons have an ownership interest in, or any affiliation with, another ATC or IATA approved travel agency not listed in Part I above? . . . . ☐ YES ☐ NO
If so, give name of such person(s), the name and address of the agency, and describe the affiliation:

D. Is there any one client or customer, including companies, entities or persons, with whom you have done, or expect to do, 20% or more of your gross annual air transportation business? . . . . ☐ YES ☐ NO

If so, does such client or customer, (including its officers, directors, stockholders, owners, or employees), have any ownership, financial or controlling interest in the agency; or is such client or customer controlled by, or under common control with the agency for which this application is intended? . . . . ☐ YES ☐ NO

Note: If your answer to the preceding question is "Yes," give details in Part VII of this form and refer to Section IV.L. of the enclosed excerpts to the Agency Resolution <u>before</u> submitting your application.

E. Has any person who is affiliated with the agency <u>in any capacity</u>:

(1) had a connection or affiliation with, or financial interest in, or been employed by, any agent cancelled by the Air Traffic Conference or the International Air Transport Association?. . . . . ☐ YES ☐ NO

(2) been adjudged bankrupt, or is the subject of pending bankruptcy proceedings? . . . . ☐ YES ☐ NO

(3) been convicted of a felony, or convicted of a misdemeanor related to financial activities or a breach of fiduciary duty involving the use of the funds of others? . . . . ☐ YES ☐ NO

(4) been denied application for a travel agent license by any governmental authority, or had a travel agent license suspended, revoked or cancelled by any governmental authority? . . . . ☐ YES ☐ NO

(5) Is any such person presently under suspension or pending action of any kind by the Travel Agent Commissioner? . . . . ☐ YES ☐ NO

If your answer is "Yes" to any of the above, give <u>full particulars</u> in part VII of this form.

PART III. LOCATION OF AGENCY FOR WHICH THIS APPLICATION IS INTENDED

A. Give date on which this office opened for business as a travel bureau: _____

B. Is the travel bureau open to the general public during normal business hours? . . . . ☐ YES ☐ NO
If not, explain in part VII of this form.

C. Is the business conducted at this office <u>exclusively</u> a travel agency business? . . . . ☐ YES ☐ NO

If not, give details in Part VII of this form as to how the travel bureau is separated from the other business activity.

D. Check the appropriate box if your agency is located in any one of the following: ☐ hotel; ☐ motel; ☐ private club; ☐ private residence; ☐ on property owned or utilized by an airport or airline terminal, or ☐ university or college campus.

Note: if your agency is located in one of the foregoing locations, describe the location in Part VII of this form, and review Section I.S.I.T. or IV.L of the enclosed excerpts to the Agency Resolution before submitting your application.

E. Submit photographs of the interior and exterior of the agency location along with this application (snapshots are acceptable and one set of photos is sufficient).

PART IV. QUALIFICATIONS AND JOB DESCRIPTIONS OF QUALIFIED PERSONNEL

NOTE: So that your application may be considered complete, it is essential that the following questions be answered in sufficient detail to demonstrate that the personnel experience standards set forth in Section IV.B.10 of the Agency Resolution have been met. The following explanation of these requirements is offered for your guidance:

The experience and qualification requirements of the person(s) operating the agency for which this application is intended are considered in two separate and distinct parts. The first part, posed in question A and relating only to an owner, officer or manager of the agency, requires a minimum of two years' full-time experience in creative selling, marketing and promotional activities in the sale of passenger transportation and services related thereto. This is not to be confused with experience as an "order taker" or simply servicing an already established account. The promotional experience referred to here means full-time experience in developing new travel markets —e.g., inducing people to travel who would not otherwise have done so.

The second part of the experience requirements, posed in question B, may relate to any full-time employee of the agency and covers the technical side. In this category, you need to present evidence that at least one person, employed full-time in the office for which this application is made, has had, within the past five years, a minimum of one year's experience in airline ticketing and reservations with either an ATC or IATA member airline or an ATC or IATA approved travel agency.

A. PROMOTIONAL SALES EXPERIENCE
1. List the name, resident address and home telephone number of the owner, officer or manager on whom you are relying to establish the requisite experience in creative selling, marketing and promotional activities relating to air transportation or other passenger transportation and services related thereto, and give the precise title of such person. *Note: Such person must be staffing the location for which this application is intended on a full-time, daily basis:*

_____
_____

2. Give the <u>name and address of the employer(s) or firm(s)</u> in which the person listed above acquired the necessary experience, <u>and</u> show the beginning and ending dates of employment for each. As to each, describe the capacity in which the person was employed, including title and precise duties, <u>and explain his or her activites and contributions in regard to creative selling, promoting and marketing of air transportation</u>, or other passenger transportation, and services related thereto. (Letters from such former employer(s) or co-workers attesting to the experience acquired are suggested.) Do <u>not</u> list non-travel related experience or training schools. If you wish to attach a separate resume, please submit it in <u>duplicate</u>. **THE INFORMATION PROVIDED BELOW MUST BE SUFFICIENTLY DETAILED TO DEMONSTRATE THAT THE INDIVIDUAL MEETS THE EXPERIENCE REQUIREMENTS EXPLAINED ABOVE.**

Name of Employer (firm, organization, etc.) and Address	Dates of Employment (Month/Year) From To	Title and Detailed Description of Duties

(If more space is needed, use Part VII of this form.)

Page 3

3. Has the above named person ever qualified a travel agency for ATC approval? If so, give the name of the agency, address and agency code number.

_____
_____

4. Does this person have any other occupation or employment for gainful purposes not directly connected with this agency? .... ☐ YES ☐ NO
   If so, explain in Part VII of this form.

5. If such person is <u>not</u> an owner or officer of the agency, provide the following information:

   a. Does this person have the authority to employ and discharge employees of this agency? ... ☐ YES ☐ NO

   b. Does this person have the authority to commit expenditures for such programs as advertising? ☐ YES ☐ NO

   c. Is this person authorized to sign and issue checks to cover debts incurred by the agency? .... ☐ YES ☐ NO

B. AIRLINE TICKETING & RESERVATIONS EXPERIENCE

1. Give the name of at least one person employed full-time in the office for which this application is made who has had the required minimum of one year's experience in airline ticketing and reservations within the past five years. *(Note: This person may, but need not be, the same person listed in item A.1 on the preceding page. If same, please indicate and disregard item 2. below.)*:

2. Give the name and address of the ATC or IATA approved travel agency or airline at which the experience was gained, and give the beginning and ending dates of employment. As to each, describe capacity in which employed, including title and precise duties. (Letters from former employers attesting to the employee's ability in airline ticketing and reservations are suggested). If you wish to attach a separate resume, please submit it in duplicate.

Name and Address of Employer (Travel Agency or Airline)	Dates of Employment (Month/Year) From To	Title & Duties

PART V. SECURITY FOR ATC TICKET STOCK AND AIRLINE IDENTIFICATION PLATES

By CAB Order, all applicants for ATC approval are required to furnish satisfactory evidence that they will meet the minimum safeguards for the protection of ATC ticket stock, validation plates, etc. These safeguards are outlined in Schedule B of the ATC Sales Agency Agreement and include a requirement that you obtain a bank safety deposit box or similar off-premises security facility for the storage of your reserve supply of tickets.

A. Give the name and address of the bank, or equivalent off-premises facility, with which you have made safety deposit box or other security arrangements for the storage of your excess supply of airline ticket stock: _____

B. Check which type of facility you have <u>in the agency</u> for the storage of your on-premises working supply of ticket stock and identification plates.   ☐ Locked Steel Container   ☐ Safe or Vault

PART VI. AGREEMENT

It is hereby understood and agreed that, if this application is disapproved by the Executive Secretary of ATC, the right to have the disapproval reviewed is limited to the following: (a) the applicant may request an independent review by the Travel Agent Commissioner in accordance with section IV.D.5 of the ATC agency resolution 80.10 (see enclosed excerpts), provided that the request is made to the Executive Secretary by certified mail, with a copy to the commissioner, within 30 days after receipt of the notice of disapproval; and (b) if this application is then disapproved by the commissioner, the applicant may submit the disapproval to arbitration in accordance with the terms and conditions set forth in section IV.D.6 of the ATC agency resolution 80.10 (see enclosed excerpts), and ATC and the applicant will accept as final and binding the award of the arbitral tribunal.

The Air Traffic Conference is required by the terms of its Agency Resolution as approved by Civil Aeronautics Board Order 76-5-57, to inform each disapproved applicant of the reasons for the disapproval and the basis on which it was determined that the applicant or the location in question did not meet the requirements of the Agency Resolution, or that the applicant could not be relied upon to adhere to the terms of the Sales Agency Agreement. Accordingly, the undersigned, on behalf of the applicant, expressly waives any and all claims, causes of action, or rights to recovery based upon libel, slander or defamation of character by reason of such publication of assorted grounds or reasons for disapproval of this application or for removal from the Agency List, or of alleged violations or other charges for which review of the Agent's eligibility is requested, as is reasonably related to the performance of appropriate functions specified in applicable Air Traffic Conference Resolutions.

Enter your Federal Taxpayer's Account Number here (to be obtained through your local IRS office):

IMPORTANT → _____

I hereby certify that the statements made in this application (including statements made in any attachments thereto) are true and correct, and that I am authorized by the organization identified in the answer to Part I of this questionnaire to make these statements and to file this application.

_____
Signature of Officer or Owner

State of _____

County of _____

On this _____ day of _____, 19___, _____
(Name of Officer or Owner)

appeared before me, and being first duly sworn, stated that he is the _____
(Owner or Other Title)

of _____
(Name of Travel Agency)

That, being duly authorized to do so, he executed the foregoing application on behalf of _____

_____, that the statements contained herein are true
(Name of Travel Agency)

and correct, and that it is his signature which appears above.

_____
Notary Public

My Commission expires on _____

NOTARY SEAL

THIS QUESTIONNAIRE MUST BE SUBMITTED TO THE AIR TRAFFIC
CONFERENCE IN DUPLICATE (ORIGINAL & ONE COPY).
(BE SURE TO KEEP AN EXTRA COPY FOR YOUR PERMANENT RECORD)

AIR TRAFFIC CONFERENCE
Sales Agency Agreement

(ATC—SAA—September 5, 1978 issue)

1. Effectiveness:

This Agreement shall become effective as between the Agent and each air carrier, which is a party to the Air Traffic Conference Agency Resolution, (hereinafter called "the Carrier") on the date stated above, unless the Carrier notifies the Agent by certified or registered mail with a copy to the Executive Secretary (such notice to be distributed to all airline participants) that the Agent shall not represent that Carrier. This Agreement shall have the same force and effect between the Carrier and the Agent as though they were both named herein and as though they had subscribed their names hereto on the date appearing above.

2. Scope of the Agent's Authority and Activities:

The authority of the Agent to represent the Carrier shall be specifically limited to the authority expressly granted by this Agreement.

During the term of this Agreement, the Agent shall represent the Carrier for the purpose of promoting and selling air passenger transportation offered by the Carrier: Provided, That, the Agent shall not represent any Carrier who has notified the Agent by certified or registered mail that the Agent shall not represent the Carrier; Provided, Further, That, the Agent may elect to limit such representation to certain specific product lines of the Carriers (e.g. Advertised Air Tours, Convention Air Tours, Incentive Air Tours, Independent Air Tours, Family Travel, "Discover America" fares, charters, or point-to-point domestic air passenger transportation not included in any of the foregoing categories) if the Agent limits its representation of all carriers' services alike and so notifies the Executive Secretary in writing; and, Provided, Further, That the Agent shall not be required to sell air passenger transportation offered by the Carrier where payment therefor is to be made under the Universal Air Travel Plan and where the Agent is paid no commission by the Carrier for such sale. In selling air passenger transportation, the Agent shall conform to and observe the tariffs, rules, regulations and instructions issued by the Carrier, and the applicable terms and conditions of tickets and exchange orders of the Carrier issued or used by the Agent. The Agent shall furnish information to its clients and the public concerning the Carrier's air passenger transportation services in conformance with current authorized forms, folders, advertising, schedules, tariffs, rules, regulations and instructions issued by the Carrier.

The Agent shall exercise the authority granted by this Agreement, and represent itself as an agent of the Carrier, only at such places of business operated by the Agent as are included from time to time on the ATC Agency List maintained pursuant to the ATC Agency Resolution. Except at an authorized In-Plant location, the Agent shall not pay directly or indirectly any portion of the salary or expenses of any person regularly located on the premises of a customer, the duties of which person include the making of airline reservations or the preparation, validation or delivery of airline tickets.

The promotional and sales activities of the Agent on behalf of the Carrier shall not be restricted as to territory.

The Agent shall not knowingly or carelessly sell or issue tickets or exchange orders covering air passenger transportation offered by the Carrier to persons who plan to sell, issue, or offer to sell or issue, such transportation documents, but who have not been authorized by the Carrier to represent the Carrier. No credit card which is issued in the name of the Agent, or in the name of any of the Agent's personnel, or in the name of any third party, shall be used for the purchase of air transportation for sale or resale to other persons.

In selling air passenger transportation hereunder, the Agent shall use, in the following order of preference, the airline identification plate of air carriers which are parties to the Air Traffic Conference Agency Resolution:

a. The Carrier through which the reservation is made, provided such Carrier participates in the routing, or

b. The Carrier performing the first sector of the transportation, or

c. If the Agent does not have either plate specified above, the plate of any Carrier which is scheduled to participate in the transportation, or

d. If authorized by the Carrier, an Agent may use the identification plate of that Carrier for transportation entirely over the routes of another Carrier(s): Provided, However, That the Agent shall not use the identification plate of any Carrier for transportation entirely over the routes of any other Carrier who has notified the Agent by certified or registered mail that the Agent shall not represent that Carrier.

Any Agent ticket delivery facility established, operated or maintained, directly or indirectly on the premises of any airport or within any airport terminal building may only be used for tickets actually issued at an authorized agency location and delivered to such facility by the Agent.

The Agent is not authorized to admit, accept or receive service of summons or other process on behalf of the Carrier, any other airline participating in the ATC Standard Agent's Ticket and Area Settlement Plan, the Air Transport Association of America, or the Air Traffic Conference of America, service of legal process upon the Agent on behalf of the Carrier or any of the other above-named persons is therefore invalid and without any legal effect whatsoever.

If an Agent utilizes an outside sales representative, the following conditions shall apply:

(a) An outside sales representative cannot operate out of a separate, fixed, non-approved location;

(b) he must clearly represent himself through local advertising, business cards, stationery, etc., as a representative of the approved agent only, giving the name, address and telephone number of the authorized location. He may list his residence and/or mobile telephone number;

(c) he may operate on a commissionable basis;

(d) he need not devote full-time to agency sales, and may be gainfully employed elsewhere (does not apply to reduced rate eligibility);

(e) he cannot write, validate or issue tickets at any location other than the approved agency location;

PROVIDED, however, nothing herein shall preclude the delivery of a properly issued and validated ticket to the agency's client;

(f) the contact number given to the carrier must be the telephone number of the authorized location and pertinent reservation and booking information must be maintained at the authorized agency location.

3. Designation of Agency:

The Agent may represent himself, on letterheads, advertising, telephone listings and classifications, office signs, and otherwise, as an "Agent" or "Travel Agent" representing the Carrier, but shall not represent himself as a "General Agent" or use any other designation (such as "Air Lines Ticket Office" or "Consolidated Air Lines Ticket Office") which would indicate or imply in any way that his office is an office of the Carrier.

4. Issuance of Tickets and Exchange Orders:

In selling air passenger transportation on the lines of the Carrier, the Agent shall issue only Standard Agent's Tickets or exchange orders supplied pursuant to this Agreement, except to the extent the Carrier (1) authorizes the Agent, in writing, to draw its own exchange orders on the Carrier, (2) supplies the Agent with, and instructs the Agent to use, envelope-type exchange orders, (3) the Carrier authorizes the Agent in writing to receive standard teletype tickets in accordance with the terms and conditions of the ATC/IATA Teletype Ticketing Agreement Agents. The Agent shall deliver to its clients the proper forms of tickets or exchange orders as authorized from time to time by the Carrier; and routing information, et cetera, shown on any such documents shall be in accordance with the applicable rules, regulations and instructions furnished to the Agent by the Carrier.

Standard Agent's Ticket forms or exchange orders for issuance to the Agent's clients to cover transportation purchased will be supplied to the Agent by the senior officer of the ATA Economics and Finance Department or his designee as agent for the Carrier.

All ticket forms and exchange orders supplied by or on behalf of the Carrier to the Agent shall be held in trust by the Agent until issued to the Agent's clients to cover transportation purchased, or until otherwise satisfactorily accounted for to the Carrier, or to the senior office of the ATA Economics and Finance Department or his designee, and will be surrendered upon demand, together with all airline identification plates, to the senior office of the ATA Economics and Finance Department or his designee, or his designated representative, acting pursuant to the Air Traffic Conference Agency Resolution.

The Agent will procure, at no expense to the Carrier, one or more validator machine(s), or ticket writer(s), of a type approved by the senior officer of the ATA Economics and Finance Department or his designee, for use at each place of business covered by this Agreement in the issuance of Standard Agent's Tickets or exchange orders pursuant to instructions issued from time to time by the Carrier or the senior officer of the ATA Economics and Finance Department or his designee.

The Carrier may, at its option, provide the Agent with one or more airline identification plate(s) for use in the issuance of tickets in said validator machine or ticket writer. Such airline identification plate shall remain the property of the Carrier, and shall be returned to it upon demand or upon the termination of this Agreement as between the Agent and the Carrier.

Ticket forms and exchange orders supplied by or on behalf of the Carrier for issuance at a specified place of business covered by this Agreement shall not be written up and/or validated at any other place of business and, except as provided in Paragraph 2, shall not be delivered to customers at or through any other agency location or In-Plant location, or at or through any facility maintained, directly or indirectly, by the Agent on a Customer's premises or at any other location not an authorized agency location under the ATC Agency Resolution, nor shall an airline identification plate supplied for use at a specified place of business be used at any other place of business.

5. Reports and Settlements:

The Agent shall provide to the Executive Secretary information, and an authorization, in such forms as may be prescribed from time to time by the Executive Secretary, permitting the designated area bank to draw checks upon the Agent's trust account or other bank account in payment for sums due hereunder. Agent shall give the Executive Secretary 30 days advance notice by certified or registered mail of its intention to change banks, or bank accounts.

The Agent may submit to the designated area bank in connection with the sales report hereafter provided, a settlement limitation amount authorization in the format and in accordance with the instructions prescribed by the Executive Secretary, which sets forth the maximum amount the designated area bank is authorized to draw against the Agent's trust account or other bank account.

The Agent shall report once each week for all air transportation and ancillary services sold hereunder for which the Agent has issued Standard Agent's Ticket or exchange orders, or drawn exchange orders on the Carrier. Each such report shall include all such sales during the 7-day period, Monday through Sunday inclusive, ending midnight Sunday of that week. The report shall be in a form specified by the Executive Secretary. All tickets and other accountable documents and remittances therefor must be reported on, and be included with, the sales reports for the reporting period in which they are validated.

The Agent shall cause each such report, together with auditor's coupons and supporting documents, to be delivered to the designated area bank not later than the close of banking hours on the Tuesday following the last day of the period covered by the report or the close of banking hours on the next banking day if the Monday or Tuesday following the last day of the period covered by the report is a federal or state legal holiday, Rosh Hashanah or Yom Kippur. The Agent shall be deemed to have complied with this requirement if the envelope containing the report and supporting documents is mailed (posted) not later than midnight of the Tuesday following the last day of the period covered by the report, unless either the Monday or Tuesday following the last day of the period covered by the report is a federal or state legal holiday or Rosh Hashanah or Yom Kippur in which case the Agent shall be deemed to have complied with this requirement if the envelope is mailed not later than midnight Wednesday following the last day of the report period. Evidence of timely mailing shall not include non-Post Office postage metered mail dates but shall be limited to (1) a Post Office post mark, (2) a certificate of mailing issued by the Post Office or (3) other evidence supplied by the Post Office of the mailing date.

If no air transportation or ancillary services have been sold hereunder during such period, the Agent shall, on such form as may be prescribed from time to time by the Executive Secretary, advise the designated area bank of such no sales within the time specified above.

The report shall account, in such manner as may be described from time to time by the Executive Secretary, for all sums due the Carrier hereunder, and for all receipts and other required documents accepted by the Agent in payment for air transportation and ancillary services sold hereunder for which the Agent has issued Standard Agent's Tickets or exchange orders, or has drawn exchange orders on the Carrier pursuant to the Universal Air Travel Plan or other credit plan honored by the Carrier.

Upon reciept of the report, the designated area bank shall determine the sums due the carrier for sales during such period and shall thereupon draw a check for the sums due on the trust account or other account maintained by the Agent at the Agent's bank for such purposes, but in no event shall the check so drawn be in excess of the settlement limitation specified by the Agent, or be presented for payment earlier than the tenth day following the ending date of such period. The designated area bank shall, for each such reporting period, provide the Agent with a report of transaction, entitled Weekly Sales Summary, for the period which shall also show the amount of the check drawn on the account maintained by the Agent.

The Agent shall retain his duplicate copy of each report and his copies of supporting documents, as well as the Weekly Sales Summary, for at least two years.

Settlement of amounts due shall be made in official currency of the country in which the Agent is located, or its equivalent, unless otherwise instructed in writing by the Executive Secretary.

All moneys, less applicable commissions to which the Agent is entitled hereunder, collected by the Agent for air transportation and ancillary services sold hereunder for which the Agent has issued Standard Agent's Tickets or exchange orders or has drawn exchange orders on the Carrier, and other required documents accepted by the Agent in payment for air passenger transportation or ancillary services sold hereunder for which the Agent has issued Standard Agent's Tickets or exchange orders or has drawn exchange orders on the Carrier, pursuant to the Universal Air Travel Plan or other credit plan accepted by the Carrier, shall be the property of the carrier, and shall be held in trust by the Agent until satisfactorily accounted for to the Carrier.

No Agent may report to the Carrier the sale of any air transportation as a credit card transaction where at any time the Agent bills, invoices, or receives payment in cash from the customers for such air transportation.

The books and records of the Agent relating to the sales of air transportation and ancillary services offered by the Carrier shall be open to inspection by the Carrier and/or an auditor or other duly authorized representative of the Air Traffic Conference of America.

A "Standard Travel Agent Finance Statement", Schedule D, Supplement I, is appended hereto and incorporated herein. Such statement shall be separately executed by the Agent and the Executive Secretary of the Air Traffic Conference of America, acting as agent for the several air carriers which are parties to the Air Traffic Conference Agency Resolution and the participants in the Standard Agent's Ticket and Area Settlement Plan. The Executive's Secretary shall file such executed Statement with the appropriate authorities in the state(s) in which the Agent is doing business.

5.A. Maintenance of Bond:

The Agent, shall, without expense to the Carrier or the Air Traffic Conference of America, procure and maintain, or cause to be procured and maintained, for the joint and several benefit of the members of the Air Traffic Conference of America, a bond or bonds, conditioned upon the Agent's compliance with the provisions of this Agreement with respect to remittances to the Carrier, in a form prescribed from time to time by the Agency Committee of said Conference in the minimum amount of $10,000, such amount to be increased whenever necessary to cover the highest quarter's (of the last four) gross sales of air transportation wholly within the United Staes, divided by three, for the accounts of members of the Air Traffic Conference: Provided, That, (a) the Agent shall not be required to maintain said bond in an amount in excess of $50,000; (b) the Agent shall be relieved of the requirement to provide coverage in excess of the $10,000 minimum if:

1. the Agent is determined by the Executive Secretary to be a "Bank Travel Department" within the meaning of the Air Traffice Conference Agency Resolution, or

2. the Agent submits to the Executive Secretary annually a current balance sheet, certified by a certified public accountant to present fairly the financial position of the Agent, which establishes

that total assets available for satisfaction of debts exceed liabilities by at least $75,000, and the credit rating of the Agent, if published by Dun and Bradstreet or other recognized credit-rating agency, is shown as "good" or higher; and

3. after the Agent has been on the Air Traffic Conference Agency List for one year, adjustment of the amount of the bond to provide coverage in excess of the $10,000 minimum shall be made at least once a year, and at any other time when the amount of the Agent's bond fails by $2,000 or more to provide the required coverage. Nothing herein shall be deemed to preclude an Agent from reducing the amount of coverage whenever consideration of his sales experience for the most recent twelve consecutive months shows him to be carrying a bond in excess of that herein required.

6. Misrepresentation as to Routing, et cetera:

The Agent shall not make any misrepresentation as to the Carrier, aircraft, or route by which any passenger is to be transported, nor as to any service to be furnished by the Carrier.

7. Securing of Accommodations:

The Agent shall request reservation of space only when the Agent has had a request to do so from a client and, if so required by the Carrier, when a deposit therefor in the proper amount has been paid to the Agent by the client. The Agent when requested shall provide the Carrier with the passenger's contact address or telephone number, if available, and shall secure confirmation from the Carrier that a definite reservation has been made before issuance to the client of a ticket or exchange order for any particular flight or flights. Tickets within the established ticketing time limits and exchange orders shall always be issued strictly in accordance with the reservation status of each flight section involved as advised by the Carrier concerned; except that, unless otherwise instructed by the Carrier, an exchange order may be issued to a client covering "open date" transportation, or a ticket may be so issued which includes an "open date" section(s) for which no space has been reserved at the time of issuance to the client, provided such forms or tickets are properly marked to indicate "open date" issuance in accordance with current instructions of the Carrier.

All reservations for a specific itinerary and changes thereto shall be requested through one Carrier. The Agent shall refrain from making duplicate reservations for the same passenger except in those circumstances where the Agent is unable to secure confirmation of space on the Carrier of flight of the client's choice in which case a "protective reservation" may be made. Such a reservation must be identified as such to the Carrier(s).

When making reservations for a group, the Agent shall strictly adhere to the time-limits established by a Carrier for notification of passenger names and recall of unused space. When a Carrier is unable to confirm the required number of seats for a group, the Agent shall not subsequently obtain the seats by requesting several individual reservations.

The Agent shall advise the Carrier concerned of any subsequent changes to a reservations request making sure to cancel and release all space not required.

8. Remuneration—Commission:

As remuneration for the services performed by the Agent hereunder, the Carrier agrees, subject to the limitations set forth in this Agreement, to pay the Agent as commission a percentage (as set forth in Schedule A attached hereto and made a part hereof) of the fares and charges applicable to the air passenger transportation offered by the Carrier which is sold by the Agent hereunder. Such commission shall be accepted by the Agent as full compensation for its services rendered to the Carrier hereunder. No commission will be paid to the Agent for the sale of any air passenger transportation unless;

1. such Agent issued a ticket or an exchange order covering the air passenger transportation for the sale of which the commission is paid, and

2. such Agent collected the proper amount of fares and charges applicable to such transportation or procured a properly executed transportation receipt and other documents as required pursuant to the Universal Air Travel Plan.

Provided, That, this shall not preclude payment of commission in connection with a charter when such Agent is designated to represent the charterer in the charter contract and the charterer has paid the Carrier directly.

No commission will be paid to the Agent for the sale of any air passenger transportation solely over the lines of any Carrier who has notified the Agent by certified or registered mail that the Agent shall not represent that Carrier.

The Agent shall not be entitled to a commission for the sale of any air passenger transportation, and shall refund any commission previously paid or retained in connection with such sale, unless the passenger is actually transported by the Carrier to a point other than that at which he embarks; except that, where the terms of sale of the transportation provide for a return to the point of embarkation without landing at any other point, the Agent shall be entitled to a commission if the passenger is actually transported in accordance with such terms.

In cases of cancellation by the Agent's client of any portion of the transportation sold by the Agent and for which the Agent has issued a ticket or exchange order supplied by or on behalf of the Carrier or has drawn an exchange order on the Carrier, the Agent shall not be entitled to a commission for the sale of the portion so cancelled, and shall, on demand of the Carrier, refund any commission previously paid or retained in connection with such sale.

No commission will be paid to the Agent for the sale of any air passenger transportation for which the Agent issues a ticket (or portion thereof) or exchange order in violation of any provisions of this Agreement.

No commission will be paid to the Agent for the sale of any air passenger transportation, exclusively between points in the Continental United States and/or Canada, which is paid for under the Universal Air Travel Plan; *Provided*, That if such Plan is entered into after the sale was made, a commission will be paid on such sale as if no such Plan had been entered into; and *Provided, Further,* That nothing herein shall prohibit payment of commission at the regular rate on the tariff fares and charges applicable to the domestic air passenger transportation:

1. included in an Advertised Air Tour, Convention Air Tour, Incentive Air tour, and Independent Air Tour, or
2. for the sale of any ticket for Family Travel, as provided by Section VIII.D.6, Resolution 80.10, or
3. for the sale of any ticket for travel at "Discover America" excursion fares, as provided by Section VIII.D.7, Resolution 80.10.

No commission will be paid to the Agent for the sale of any air passenger transportation paid for by Government travel voucher, warrant, or similar Government purchase contract.

No commission will be paid to the Agent for the sale of any air transportation for which the Agent issues a ticket or exchange order to the Agent or to any person(s) which owns, controls, is controlled by, is under common control with, or has a financial interest in, the Agent, or to any officer, director or employee of the aforementioned person(s). *Provided,* That this subparagraph shall not preclude payment of commission because of a financial interest arising from investment in an Agent which is an entity whose shares are listed on a securities exchange or are regularly traded in an over-the-counter market; and *Provided, Further,* That this subparagraph shall not preclude payment of commission in those cases where an employee of the Agent purchases transportation for his own personal use, e.g., a vacation.

To the extent permitted by the Federal Aviation Act and the Civil Aeronautics Board acting thereunder, nothing herein shall preclude an Agent from collecting a service charge from the Customer for any services rendered or expenses incurred in connection with the sale of any air passenger transportation; Provided, That, such service charge is not included in the fare nor shown in any manner on airline ticket(s) or exchange order(s), and is separately stated in writing to the Customer.

9. Communications:

The Carrier will not accept collect telegrams or telephone calls from the Agent for any purpose, nor will the Carrier assume or pay any telephone, telegraph, mailing, printing or other communications, advertising or promotional expense of the Agent for any purpose. The Carrier will, however, prepay reservation confirmation messages to the Agent.

10. Refunds:

The Agent may refund any fare or charge applicable to air transportation sold by the Agent hereunder and for which the Agent has issued a ticket or exchange order supplied by or on behalf of the Carrier. The Agent shall make refund only to the person authorized to receive the refund and in accordance with the tariffs, rules, regulations and instructions issued by the Carrier, and shall not assess or withhold from the refund payee any amount as a service charge or otherwise. The Agent hereby agrees to indemnify and hold the Carrier harmless from and against any claim arising from the failure of the Agent to refund promptly to the authorized refund payee the proper amount of fare or other charges. If the amount refundable was collected by the Agent and remitted to the Carrier prior to making the refund, the Carrier shall reimburse the Agent the amount of such refund upon receipt of the Agent's written statement that the refund has been paid.

11. Commissions Not to Be Divided:

The Agent shall retain the full amount of the commissions allowed by the Carrier and shall not rebate or promise to rebate directly or indirectly in any manner whatsoever such commissions, or portion thereof to any passenger or client or disburse such commission or portion thereof to any person except as provided hereunder:

a. The Agent may distribute commissions to another agent;

b. Nothing herein shall preclude disbursement by the Agent of part of the commissions paid to it by the Carrier to an employee.

12. Free or Reduced Rate Transportation Furnished to Agent Not Transferable:

The Agent shall not sell or otherwise transfer any ticket or other document for air passenger transportation, issued free or at a reduced rate to him or any of his officers or employees, or for a tour conductor as defined by applicable tariffs, when such free or reduced rate ticket or document has been requested by the Agent and furnished by the Carrier without charge or at a reduced rate in accordance with the provisions of applicable tariffs and resolutions.

13. Compliance with Tariffs, Rules, Regulations and Instructions:

The Agent shall comply with all instructions of the Carrier, including any specific instructions applying to any particular case or circumstances, and shall make no representation or statement not previously authorized by the Carrier. The Agent shall deliver to the Carrier such specific instructions, requests, or particulars in connection with a client or his transportation as may be proper to enable the Carrier to render efficient service to its passengers. The Agent also agrees to adhere to and comply with the tariffs, rules, and regulations of the Carriers.

14. Advertising and Publicizing the Carrier's Services:

In carrying out the services specified hereunder and within the limitations hereof, the Agent shall make known the services of the Carrier in every way reasonably practicable. However, samples of all advertising matter to be issued by and at the expense of the Agent, in which reference is made to the Carrier, shall be approved by the Carrier prior to display or distribution thereof.

The Carrier shall furnish the Agent with timetables, schedules of fares, and other information and instructions, including advertising and publicity matter, which the Carrier customarily supplies to its Agents, and the Agent shall make effective use thereof in publicizing the services of the Carrier.

In its tour advertising of Carrier(s) services, the Agent shall comply with the "Travel Agent Tour Advertising Code," Schedule "C" of this Agreement.

15. Default:

Airline debit memos sent to the Agent are payable by the Agent upon receipt thereof.

If at any time the Agent fails to pay such debit memo, or is otherwise in default to the Carrier or to any other party to the Air Traffic Conference Agency Resolution, the carrier, at its option, may either:

a. terminate this Agreement, as between it and the Agent, by notice in writing to the Agent, such notice to take effect immediately upon its receipt; or

b. withdraw its airline identification plate from the Agent and revoke any authorization previously given to the Agent to draw its own exchange orders on the Carrier for such periods as it deems advisable and the senior officer of the ATA Economics and Finance Department or his designee may, for such periods as he deems advisable, withdraw all standard agent forms and exchange orders supplied to the Agent; or

c. forward any debit memo for which payment has not been made to the Central Collective Service pursuant to the conditions of Resolution 80.13. The Agent shall within 30 days of receipt pay all debit memos transmitted to it by the Central Collection Service. In the event the Agent shall fail to pay or contest such debit memo, the Executive Secretary shall, in accordance with the provisions of Section VII.J. of the Agency Resolution, terminate this Agreement and remove the Agent from the Agency List.

16. Adequate Amount of Business:

The Agent shall endeavor to create and stimulate the sale of air passenger transportation offered by the Carrier, to perform and provide adequate service to the Agent's clients, and to transact a sufficient amount of business to justify the costs and responsibilities incurred by the Carrier in retaining the agency. The failure or inability of the Agent to produce an amount of business sufficient to justify the continuance of the agency may result in its termination at any time by the Carrier.

17. Maintenance of Ethical Business Standards:

The Agent shall at all times maintain ethical standards of business in the conduct of the agency and in its dealing with its clients, the public and the Carrier.

17.a. Security of Ticket Stock and Airline Plates:

The Agent shall comply with the minimum safeguards to protect airline ticket stock, MCO's, identification plates and other standard ticket forms contained in Schedule "B" attached hereto. Failure to do so will constitute a breach of this Agreement, and will subject the Agent to review by the Commissioner pursuant to Resolution 80.4.

18. Liability:

a. The Carrier hereby agrees to indemnify and hold harmless the Agent, its officer, agents and employees from all responsibility and liability for any damage, expense, or loss to any person or thing caused by or arising from any negligent act or omission of the Carrier, its representatives, agents, employees, or servants, and related directly or indirectly to any transportation sold by the Agent hereunder and performed, or to be performed, by the Carrier. The Agent likewise agrees to indemnify and hold harmless the Carrier, its officers, agents and employees from all responsibility and liability for any damage, expense, or loss to any person or thing caused by or arising from any negligent act, omission, or misrepresentation of the Agent, its representatives, agents, employees, or servants. The Agent further agrees to indemnify and hold harmless the Carrier, its officers, agents and employees, from any and all damage, expense, or loss on account of the loss, misapplication, theft, or forgery of tickets, exchange orders, or other supplies furnished by or on behalf of the Carrier to the Agent, or the proceeds thereof, whether or not such proceeds have been deposited in a bank, and whether or not such loss is occasioned by the insolvency of either a purchaser of such forms or documents or of a bank in which the Agent may have deposited such proceeds, and notwithstanding the fact that, under the terms of this Agreement, such proceeds are the property of the Carrier and held in trust by the

Agent; Provided, That the Agent may be relieved of liability for losses arising from the proven theft, except by the Agent or his employees, of airline ticket stock, MCO's identification plates or other accountable standard ticket forms from his premises upon a determination by the Executive Secretary that the Agent, at the time of theft, exercised reasonable care for the protection of such airline ticket stock, MCO's, identification plates or other standard ticket forms and has immediately reported the theft to the appropriate law enforcement authorities and has promptly notified the Executive Secretary of the particulars of such theft both by telephone and telegram. Reasonable care as used herein shall include, but not be limited to compliance with the minimum safeguards set forth in Schedule B attached hereto and made a part hereof. In making the determination specified herein the Executive Secretary shall rely on the findings of the Office of Enforcement and/or cooperating security officers of Members. If it is determined that the Agent did not exercise reasonable care, the Executive Secretary shall inform the Agent of the exact manner in which the Agent has failed to exercise reasonable care and the specific details of such failure.

b. If the Agent refuses to surrender all ticket forms and exchange orders and airline identification plates upon demand made pursuant to Paragraph 4 of this Agreement, the Agent shall reimburse the Conference for all court costs, bond premiums, and reasonable attorneys' fees incurred by the Conference in recovering the ticket forms and exchange orders and airline identification plates through legal action, whether such action is adjudicated by a final order of the court or is settled or otherwise terminated by the parties prior to such final order.

However, the Agent will not reimburse the Conference for court costs, bond premiums, and reasonable attorneys' fees, in those cases in which the underlying cause of such litigation is subject to subsequent review by the Travel Agent Commissioner, in accordance with Resolution 80.4, until receipt of a final adverse decision of the Commissioner, or a final adverse decision by an arbitral tribunal in accordance with Paragraph 27 hereof.

19. Notices:

All notices to the Agent or to the Carrier shall be sufficient if sent by prepaid telegram or mail, addressed as each party may designate in writing during the term of this Agreement.

20. Agency Fees:

On or before June 1 of each year, the Agent shall pay to the Executive Secretary of the Air Traffic Conference of America an annual fee, applicable to the fiscal year commencing the following July 1 and ending June 30, in the amount prescribed by said Conference. In the event of termination of this Agreement by or on behalf of all parties to the Air Traffic Conference Agency Resolution, the annual fee attributable to the fiscal year in which such termination occurs shall be prorated as of the date of such termination, and, if the fee has already been paid by the Agent, the portion applicable to the period after such termination will be credited against amounts due from, or refunded to, the Agent; *Provided*, That the Agent shall not pay an annual agency fee with respect to any authorized agency location for the fiscal year in which such location is first placed upon the Air Traffic Conference Agency List.

21. Agency Bond:

The Agent shall be acceptable to the bonding company for coverage under such bond, and for such amount, as may be required by the Agency Committee of the Air Traffic Conference of America. Failure to so qualify shall immediately terminate this Agreement as between the Agent and all parties to the Air Traffic Conference Agency Resolution.

22. Transfer, Assignment, or Change of Name, Address or Personnel:

The name or names under which the activities of the Agent are conducted, or under which any of its offices are operated, shall be only such as are set forth in this Agreement, and such name or names shall not be changed except upon thirty (30) days advance written notice to the Executive Secretary of the Air Traffic Conference: Provided, That if within such thirty (30) days period the Executive Secretary notifies the Agent that the proposed name or names would violate Paragraph 3 of this Agreement, the change of name shall not be made.

The location of any place of business covered by this Agreement shall not be changed except upon thirty (30) days advance written notice to the Executive Secretary of the Air Traffic Conference, accompanied by evidence, satisfactory to the Executive Secretary, the new location qualifies under the terms of the ATC Agency Resolution and upon receipt of notice from the Executive Secretary that such location will be approved. In such event, the Agent shall complete and execute such form or forms as may be required by the Agency Committee to reflect the change of location. If the Executive Secretary determines that such location fails to qualify under the terms of the ATC Agency Resolution, he shall not approve the change and shall notify the Agent accordingly, setting forth the reasons therefor. The Agent shall have the right to obtain review of such decision by the Commissioner pursuant to the provisions of Resolution 80.4. Provided, that the Agent may nevertheless change the location pending determination by the Commissioner as to whether the location is qualified.

This Agreement shall not be assignable or otherwise transferable by the Agent, nor shall any interest in the shares of stock of the Agent be sold or otherwise transferred (unless such Agent is an entity whose shares are listed on a securities exchange or are regularly traded in an over-the-counter market, or unless such single or cumulative transaction(s) involves 10% or less of the issued and outstanding shares of the stock of the Agent), except with the consent of the Executive Secretary: Provided, That temporary consent to the assignment or transfer of the Agreement, or the sale or transfer of stock, pending final action, may be given by the Executive Secretary of the Air Traffic Conference upon receipt of an application, in a form prescribed by the ATC Agency Committee, setting forth information with respect to the assignee or transferee, his financial status, and other matters bearing on his qualifications. Provided, further, That any consent, or temporary consent, to the assignment or transfer of the Agreement shall be given only on the condition that the assignor or transferor and the assignee or transferee assume joint and several responsibility for all financial obligations of the assignor or transferor to Carrier(s). The assignee or transferee shall be charged with any later remittances, recorded by ATC against the assignor or transferor. Such application must be received by the Executive Secretary at least 45 days in advance of the assignment or transfer of interest. The Executive Secretary shall not approve any such application where investigation reveals, or he otherwise has reason to believe, that such applicant fails to meet the requirements of the ATC Agency Resolution, and shall so advise the applicant in writing and the reasons therefor. The Executive Secretary shall promptly thereafter refer the matter to the Commissioner for review, pursuant to the provisions of Resolution 80.4. Provided, further, however, That this agreement shall not be deemed to nullify or abridge to any extent the rights and privileges of any person under the Bankruptcy Act, 11 U.S.C. 1 et seq.

The Agent shall promptly, but not later than 30 days thereafter, notify the Executive Secretary of the Air Traffic Conference whenever the Agent fails to meet the personnel experience standards specified in paragraph IV.B.10. of the Agency Resolution at any location(s) included under this Agreement. (Note: Paragraph IV.B.10. of the Agency Resolution sets forth specific experience qualifications required for inclusion and retention on the Agency List.)

23. Other Agreements Superseded:

This Agreement shall supersede any and all prior agreements between the Agent and any party to the Air Traffic Conference Agency Resolution concerning the sale of air passenger transportation offered by any such party, except with respect to rights and liabilities existing at the date hereof.

24. Termination:

This Agreement may be terminated as between the Agent and the Carrier, at any time by notice in writing from either to the other, such notice to take effect immediately upon its receipt, subject to the fulfillment by each of all obligations accrued prior to the receipt of such notice. This Agreement may be terminated as between the Agent and all parties to the Air Traffic Conference Agency Resolution, at any time by notice in writing from the Agent to the Executive Secretary of the Air Traffic Conference of America, or from the Executive Secretary of the said Conference (or his authorized representative) to the Agent, such notice to take effect immediately upon its receipt, subject to the fulfillment by the Agent, and by each party to the said Resolution of all obligations accrued prior to the receipt of such notice. Upon termination of this Agreement as between the Agent and the Carrier, the airline identification plate shall immediately be returned to the Carrier, together with all moneys due and payable to the Carrier hereunder, and a complete and satisfactory accounting rendered. Upon termination of this Agreement as between the Agent and parties to the Air Traffic Conference Agency Resolution, all unused Standard Agent's Ticket forms and exchange orders shall immediately be returned to the senior officer of the ATA Economics and finance Department or his designee, and all airline identification plates shall immediately be returned to the Carrier, together with all moneys due and payable to the Carrier hereunder, and a complete and satisfactory accounting rendered.

25. Rights, etc. of Air Carriers Several:

The rights, powers, privileges, immunities, and duties under this Agreement, of the air carriers which are parties to the Air Traffic Conference Agency Resolution shall be several and not joint.

26. Subject to Carrier's Obligations, etc., under Air Traffic Conference Agency Resolution:

The Agent recognizes that the Carrier is party to the Air Traffic Conference Agency Resolution and as such is entitled to certain rights and is subject to certain obligations under the provisions of said Resolution. The Agent further recognizes that this Agreement is entered into for an indefinite period and that it may be terminated at any time by the Carrier, as provided in Paragraph 24 hereof, for any reason deemed sufficient by the Carrier, and that the Carrier is under no obligation to justify such termination. The Agent agrees that this Agreement and the rights and obligations of the parties hereto are subject to the said Air Traffic Conference Agency Resolution and the rights and obligations of the Carrier thereunder, and that the Agent shall have no recourse against the Carrier, or the Air Traffic Conference of America, or any member of the Air Traffic Conference of America, or against any officer, employee, agent or servant of any of them, by reason of any action taken in accordance with the provisions of the said Resolution, or by any reason of any termination of this Agreement in accordance with its provisions.

27. Arbitration:

Any claim or controversy arising out of, or relating to, any action of the Commissioner shall be settled by arbitration of the following terms and conditions:

a. *Selection of Arbiters:*
Within 30 days after receipt by Agent of the decision of the Commissioner in any review proceeding under Resolution 80.4, the Agent shall notify the Executive Secretary by certified or registered mail if he desires to have such decision reviewed by an arbitral tribunal and shall, at the same time, name one arbiter acceptable to the Agent. Such notice shall enclose the amount of $100.00 as a deposit toward the Agent's share of the expenses of arbitration. Within 10 days after receipt of such notice from Agent, the Executive Secretary shall name an arbiter acceptable to the Executive Secretary, notifying Agent by certified or registered mail of the person so selected. Within 20 days after mailing of such notice by the Executive Secretary, the two arbiters so selected shall designate a third, who shall serve as chairman of the tribunal. If such third arbiter shall not have been designated within 90 days after date of mailing by the Executive Secretary of notice that the Agent has been removed, such third arbiter shall be designated by the American Arbitration Association.

b. *Conduct of Appeal:*
The tribunal so selected shall set the matter down for the hearing not later than 30 days after selection of the chairman and shall notify the Executive Secretary and the Agent of the time and place of such hearing by registered mail: Provided, That at the request of the Agent the date of the hearing may be postponed until after the next review by the Commissioner so as to permit him to reconsider his prior decision. In the conduct of proceedings before the tribunal, the rules and procedures of the American Arbitration Association, insofar as they are applicable, and not in conflict with this Resolution shall govern. The decision of a majority of the arbiters shall be final and binding upon the Agent and the parties to the Air Traffic Conference Agency Resolution. The expenses of arbitration, including any fees payable to the arbiters, shall be shared equally by the Agent and the Conference.

c. *Scope of Appeal:*
Review by the arbitral tribunal shall be appellate and not de novo. The tribunal shall affirm the decision of the Commissioner unless it finds and concludes that the Commissioner's decision is deficient in one or more of the following respects:

(i) it is not supported by substantial evidence;

(ii) new evidence is available to the tribunal which for good cause was not presented to the Commissioner;

(iii) it contains errors of applicable law;

(iv) it is arbitrary or capricious;

(v) it is not in accordance with the terms of this Resolution or Resolution 80.4; or

(vi) the penalty is inappropriate, inadequate or excessive.

d. *Status Pending Arbitration:*

Upon or prior to notifying the Executive Secretary that he demands arbitration, the Agent shall surrender the airline identification plates to each party to the Air Traffic Conference Agency Resolution, and to the senior officer of the ATA Economics and Finance Department or his designee, all Standard Agent's Ticket forms and exchange orders supplied to the Agent, unless he posts with the Executive Secretary a bond (or a supplement to any pre-existing bond furnished under Paragraph 5.a. hereof), in an amount not less than the Agent's highest sales of air transportation commissionable hereunder in any one of the 12 preceding calendar months, expressly conditioned upon remittance in full, less applicable commission during the pendency of arbitration. During the pendency of such arbitration. Agent may continue to sell air transportation in accordance with the terms and conditions of the Agreement. If the Agent posts the bond hereinabove referred to, the senior office of the ATA Economics and Finance Department or his designee shall continue to supply Agent with Standard Agent's Ticket forms and exchange orders, and each Carrier which had supplied the Agent with airline identification plates prior to cancellation shall continue to supply him with such plates, and said remittance shall be made in accordance with the procedures prescribed in Paragraph 5 hereof.

If the Agent does not post said bond, full remittance less commissions shall be made for such transportation prior to or upon the issuance of tickets, through the use of envelope-type Air Transportation Exchange Orders or such other arrangements as may be agreed upon. Remittance shall be by legal tender, money order, cashier's check or certified check.

28. Waiver of Libel by Reason of Notice of Reasons for Review or Removal from Agency List:

The Agent recognizes that the Civil Aeronautics Board requires either the Executive Secretary, Director, Office of Enforcement, Agency Committee and/or the Commissioner as circumstances dictate, to give notice to the Agent of reasons for action taken on the Agent in the event the Commissioner or Agency Committee determines, after review of his eligibility, to remove him from the Agency List or to take such other action as the Commissioner deems appropirate, and also to give Agents upon whom review is requested for violations or other charges notice thereof. The Agent hereby expressly waives any and all claims, causes of action, or rights to recovery based upon libel, slander or defamation of character by reason of such publication of asserted grounds or reasons for removal from the Agency List or such other action which may have been prescribed, or of alleged violations or other charges for which review of the Agent's eligibility is requested, as is reasonably related to the performance of appropriate functions specified in applicable Air Traffic Conference Resolutions.

SCHEDULE A

RATES OF COMMISSION

1. For the sale of any:

    (a) Advertised Air Tour, eleven per cent (11%) of the tariff fares and charges applicable to the domestic air passenger transportation included in such tour, other than the tariff fares and charges applicable to the intra-Hawaii portion of such transportation which shall be commissionable at ten per cent (10%);

    (b) Convention Air Tour, ten per cent (10% of the tariff fares and charges applicable to the domestic air passenger transportation included in such tour; Provided, That prior to the date on which such Advertised Air Tour or Convention Air Tour is offered for sale to the

SCHEDULE D

SUPPLEMENT I, RESOLUTION 80.15
STANDARD TRAVEL AGENT FINANCE STATEMENT

1. For value received in the form of accreditation to act as Agent for the several air carriers which are parties to the Air Traffic Conference Standard Agent's Ticket and Area Settlement Plan, and in recognition of the Agent's position as trustee for such parties with respect to the proceeds derived from the sale of air transportation and ancillary services sold pursuant to the Sales Agency Agreement, until satisfactorily accounted for, _____, hereinafter called "the Agent",
(Name of Agent)
having its principal location at _____, hereby assigns, transfers and grants a security interest in the following described collateral to the Air Traffic Conference of America, having its principal location at 1709 New York Avenue, N.W., Washington, D.C. 20006, hereinafter called "the Secured Principal".

All accounts receivable and other rights to the payment of moneys which are due or which may become due to the Agent from the sale of air transportation and ancillary services issued on standard ticket forms for carriers participating in the Standard Agent's Ticket and Area Settlement Plan, less applicable sales commissions, pursuant to the Sales Agency Agreement as presently constituted and as may be hereinafter amended, including subsequent revisions and reissues thereof:

DATE	DESCRIPTION OF CONTRACT	AMOUNT DUE OR TO BECOME DUE
May 20, 1974 (including subsequent amendments thereto and revisions and reissues thereof)	Air Traffic Conference Sales Agency Agreement	All proceeds from the sale of air transportation and ancillary services issues on ATC standard ticket forms for carriers participating in the Standard Agent's Ticket and Area Settlement Plan, less applicable sales commissions, under the Contract which have not been properly remitted to the Secured Principal.

Such accounts receivable and other rights to payment which arise in the future under the aforesaid Standard Ticket Plan and Sales Agency Agreement, are hereinafter called the "Accounts" and this agreement is hereinafter called the "Contract".

2. This assignment is made as collateral security for all liabilities of the Agent to the Secured Principal under the Contract, whether now existing or hereafter arising, joint or several, due or to become due, hereinafter called the "Obligations".

3. Upon a default in the payment when due of any obligation arising under the Sales Agency Agreement, or upon the institution of bankruptcy, insolvency, liquidation or receivership proceedings or the filing of a petition for reorganization under the Bankruptcy Act by the Agent or against the Agent, or upon assignment for the benefit of creditors, all of the Obligations arising out of the Sales Agency Agreement shall become due and payable forthwith upon demand by the Secured Principal in addition to such rights and remedies as are provided herein or in any other agreement executed by the Agent. The requirement of reasonable notice of disposition of any Accounts by the Secured Principal shall be met if such notice is mailed, postage prepaid, to the address of the Agent shown at the beginning of this agreement.

4. The Agent does further agree to jointly execute a U.S.C.C. 1 security agreement with the Secured Principal and to permit the Secured Principal to file such agreement with the appropriate governmental authorities and to authorize the Secured Principal to automatically extend said filing in the event that it expires during any period in which the Agent remains accredited by the Secured Principal.

(INFORMATION COPY ONLY)

5. The Agent shall pay to the Secured Principal, on demand, any and all expenses, including legal expenses and reasonable attorney's fees, incurred or paid by the Secured Principal in protecting or enforcing any Obligations hereunder and all other rights of the Secured Principal. Such liability shall be one of the Obligations hereby secured.

6. In every instance, except where the context hereof otherwise requires, each reference to the Secured Principal and to the Agent shall be deemed to include their respective heirs, successors and assigns and each reference to the Contract shall be deemed to include all extensions, amendments, reissuances and supplements thereto.

Signed and Delivered this _____ day of _____, 19 ____.

_____ _____ Agent

Secured Principal

By _____ By _____

Acting as agent for the several airlines which are parties to the Air Traffic Conference Agency Resolution and the participants in the ATC Standard Agent's Ticket and Area Settlement Plan.

(Name)

_____

(Title)

(ATC—SAA—September 5, 1978 Issue)
(Supersedes ATC—SAA—May 20, 1974
Issue and Amendments 1, 2 and 3
thereof)

(INFORMATION COPY ONLY)

INDEX

Abbreviations, 14, 19-22
Accounting, 26, 39, 55
Agency List, 19
Airline Conferences, 15, 20
Airline Rep, 19
Air Travel Sales, 65, 75
Agency Sales Agreements, 26, 106-117
AMTRAK, 19
Appointments, application for throughout Manual, esp. 19, 37, 39, 44, 71, 79, 91-93, 95-100
   checklist for assembling, 79
Area Bank, 19, 54
ARTA (Association of Retail Travel Agents), 19, 77, 85
Associations, 90
ASTA (American Society of Travel Agents), 19, 77, 85
ATC (Air Traffic Conference), throughout Manual, esp. 15, 16, 19, 24, 25, 30-34, 37, 71, 79, 91-93, 95-100
ATC Application for Appointment, 101-105

Banks, 54, 55
Bibliography 81-84
Bond, bonding, 19, 24, 26, 44
Bonding Companies, 24, 87
Books, Sources of, 26, 81-84, 87
Bookkeeping, 61, 66
Brochures, 54, 61, 62, 87-89
Budget, 43
   checklist for planning, 48

CAB (Civil Aeronautics Board), 19
Capital, estimating need, 27
   checklist for estimating, 45
Conferences, 20, 87
Consultants, use of 27
   addresses, 87

Corporation, 40, 44
CTC (Certified Travel Counselor), 20, 77, 85

Definitions and abbreviations, 14, 19-22
Display Supplies & Equipment, 62, 88

Education, 85, 86
Employees
   contracts, 53
   checklist for evaluating, 58, 59
ERP ("experience requirement person(s)"), 20, 42, 49, 52, 53
Errors & omissions insurance, 20, 40, 88
Exchange order, 20
Expenses, recording, 36

Fam trips (familiarization), 20
Federal Employment Number, 26, 44
File cabinets, 25, 60, 69, 70
Filing systems, 25, 61, 66
Financial, need for advice, 26, 39
   commitments, 43
   requirements for appointment, 16, 48, 91, 92, 118, 119

Glossary, 14, 19-22
Guides (references), 87-89
Guidebooks, 87-89

IATA (International Air Transport Association), throughout esp. 15, 16, 20, 24, 25, 37, 63
IATA Application for 73, 74, 79, 91-92
ICTA (Institute of Certified Travel Agents), 20, 85, 77
Information, recording, 25, 35, 36
   sources and resources, 29, 87-90

121

Incorporation, 40, 44
Index, 121
Insurance, 54
IPSA (International Passenger Ship Association), 20, 76

Lawyers, 26, 39
Lease, 53
Legal Advice, 26, 39
   structure for agency, 40, 44
Libraries, use of, 24, 35, 36
Licensing, 26, 85
Location, 49, 50, 51, 91, 92
   checklist for evaluating, 56, 57
   checklist for remodeling, 60
Logo, 43, 54

Mailing lists, 66
Magazines, trade, 26, 90
Marketing, 49, 50, 56, 57 (App.A)
Mechanized reporting, 21, 77
Media, 21, 62, 63
Name for agency, 43, 54
National RR Passenger Corp. (AMTRAK), 19

Office, design, operation
   55, 61, 62, 65, 67, 76, 77, 78, 87-89
   checklists: 56, 57, 60, 69, 70
Open House, 67

Partners, 41, 42
Partnerships, 40, 41, 42, 44
Partnership agreements, 42, 44, 46, 47
Personnel, 49, 50, 51, 52, 91, 92, 94
   checklist for evaluating, 58, 59
Policies & procedures, 61, 65
Preface, 11, 12

Premises, 21, 49, 50, 51, 91, 92
   checklist for evaluating, 56, 57
   checklist for remodeling, 60
Principals, 21, 61, 62
Promotion, 88, 91, 92
Proprietorship, 40
Pros and cons of travel agency ownership, 14, 15

Reading list, 35, 36, 81-84
References, and guides, 21, 61, 62, 87-89
Retail Travel Agency, 21
RRT (reduced rate travel), 21, 77

Sales Agency Agreement, 106-117
Sales operations, 54, 61, 62, 65, 75
   checklist for setting up, 69-70
SBA (Small Business Administration), 28, 84
Sales Promotion, 62, 63, 64
Security, 54, 55
Staff, 49, 50, 51, 52, 94
   checklist for evaluating, 58, 59

Tariff, 21
Taxes, 26
Testing, 85
Tour operators, 21
TPPC (Transpacific Passenger Conference), 21, 76
Trade associations, 90
Trade publications, 26, 90
Travel agency
   definition of, 14
   general requirements for appointment, 15, 16, 18
   pros and cons of ownership, 14
   worth of, 46, 47

USTOA (U.S. Tour Operators Association), 21

ORDER BLANK

TO: FREELANCE PUBLICATIONS
      P.O. Box 8
      Bayport, N.Y. 11705

Please send me (   ) copies of TRAVEL AGENCY: A How-to-do-It Manual for Starting One of Your Own, at $9.50 per copy, postpaid.

        2-3 copies, 20% discount
        4 or more copies, 40% discount

Name _____

Address _____

_____

Payment must accompany order.